100% FINANCING!
When Buying Real Estate

by

William Joseph and
Kevin Vaughan

EATON PUBLISHING LTD., Tinley Park, IL

Eaton Publishing Ltd.,
P.O. Box 729, Tinley Park, IL 60477
(312) 479-2345

ISBN 0-9610904-0-5

10 9 8 7 6 5 4 3 2

Designed by USAd, Chicago

Printed in the United States of America

The authors have prepared this text with a high degree of accuracy. A great deal of care has been taken to provide current information. However, the ideas, general principals, suggestions, tax consequences and conclusions presented in this book are subject to local, state and federal laws and regulations. The reader is thus urged to consult legal counsel regarding any points of law, and an accountant regarding accounting procedures. This book should not be used as a substitute for advice in the foregoing professional areas.

100% FINANCING!
When Buying Real Estate

Table of Contents

Chapter Five: ZEROING IN
Selecting Your Buy

Chapter Six: FINANCING
Doing It Conventionally

Chapter Seven: CREATIVE FINANCING
Doing It With The Seller

Chapter Eight: CONTRACTS
Reading And Writing Fine Print

Acknowledgements

This book would not have been possible without
the help and support of many people, and the
authors would like to extend their thanks to all of
them; to Lois Ann, Kevin's loving and supportive
wife; to Patrick and Marianne Vaughan, Raymond
and Jewel Legreid, Mary and Lela; and to
Richard P. Allen, for so generously sharing
his accounting expertise.

They would also like to express their gratitude
to Enid Levinger Powell for her invaluable
help in writing this book.

Bill says special thanks to God,
and to his family for being able to
write this book.

PREFACE
Why Real Estate?

PREFACE
Why Real Estate?

It's hard enough to make money—but it's even harder to save it. And once you've saved it, how do you invest it to make it grow? Unless your money makes money, taxes and inflation will eat it up. So what is the average wage earner to do?

Well, let's suppose you saved $1,000 and put it in a money market fund or certificate of deposit, and were fortunate enough to receive 15% interest. You would receive $150 at the end of one year. Or would you? Let's look at the numbers:

First of all, you'll owe taxes on that $150, about 20%, or even 50% depending on your tax bracket. So there goes $30. Then inflation of 10% to 15% takes its toll—not only from the $150, but from the original $1,000. So there goes around $120 to $180, in buying power. That means that what you would have bought with that $1,000 has gone up in price over $100. So you either can't afford it now, or you will have to come up with more cash. So every year you save, and every year you are either back where you started, or a little more behind.

What did the bank do with your money? Invested it—probably in some form of real estate.

Of course you could have tried stocks. Some of them increased in value, and some did better than inflation. Some did not. Can you pick the right ones? The expert money managers of mutual funds have made their share of bad choices. Will any of them or the companies they invested in guarantee a return? No. Just for comparison's sake, ask anyone if he would sell his house for what he originally paid. Then ask if he would sell his stock for its original price. You already know his answer. Most people expect to get more for their homes now. And most would be glad to break even on their stocks or bonds.

If you are wary of companies over which you have no control, maybe you think you'd like to own your own company. O.K. First you have to invest everything you own, and borrow the rest. Second, you have to be ready to work whatever number of hours it takes a day, and days a week. Third, 50% of small businesses fail in the first two years; 80% fail in eight years. Now you know why banks don't like to invest in small companies. They prefer real estate.

You can put your money into insurance policies, but the retirement plan you set up is based on today's cost of living. You know it's going to cost more to live in the future—but how much more? What do the insurance companies do with your money? They invest in real estate.

You might consider gold, silver, diamonds, and Las Vegas. If you buy enough, hold it long enough, and sell it for more than you paid for it, you might protect your future, or your grandchildren's future. But you won't make a dime while it's in your possession. In fact, you'll pay storage and insurance costs. Las Vegas supplies the same thrill of speculation in a shorter amount of time. Most people in Las Vegas make their money investing in real estate—the hotels.

What does real estate offer that other types of investments do not? Control. Assuming you would make the same effort to learn proper methods of buying and selling, as you would make for any other investment, real estate offers the following:

1. **Conrol of risk**
   Real estate is *not* speculation. Your own efforts—not the vagaries of the market, can determine your success.

2. **Constant demand**
   There is only so much land available, and a growing population, resulting in a shortage of apartments in most communities.

3. **Profit four ways—now and in the future.**
   Appreciation—buildings gain in value due to increased rents and inflation.

   Tax Shelter—depreciation reduces current taxes; later profits on a sale are taxed at lower, capital gains rate.

   Equity—mortgage debt is gradually reduced, and equity grows.

   Cash flow—often tax-free after expenses and depreciation.

4. **Control of timing**
   Buy and sell when *you* decide, at a price *you* set, on *your* terms. You are not subject to outside forces beyond your control because:

   A. You can *show* income appreciation.

B. You can *prove* comparative value.

C. You can *count on* continued inflation.

5. **Control of financing and leverage**

Real estate lets you use other people's money through 100% Financing.

None of this information is a secret. That's why almost everyone already agrees that real estate is the best investment for the majority of people. All that prevents them—and probably you—from acting on their convictions is: *know-how.* They don't know *how* to find a good buy; *how* much to pay for it; *how* to manage it; *how* to sell it for a profit.

Bill Joseph and Kevin Vaughan do *know how.* Furthermore, they have tested and refined their knowledge in the only way that counts: they have used it successfully to buy and sell millions of dollars worth of real estate for themselves and others. They have also taught their sensible methods to thousands of average working people in seminars across the country. Their students, too, have prospered. Their most common remark, after a Joseph Seminar, has been, "Now I can see how to do it!" And then they do it!

In fact, Bill has testimonials from hundreds of his graduates who were just as timid and hopeful as he was himself when he first started. Bill Joseph grew up in a Chicago housing project. He married at 19, had three children in a row, and went to work for the Chicago Transit Authority as a bus mechanic. For twelve years he worked indoors and out, nights and weekends trying to keep up with his bills and protect his credit rating. And as he struggled, his best friend kept telling him to buy real estate "with other people's money." Bill couldn't see it.

Finally, his friend took him by the hand to buy his first apartment building—a four-flat for $28,000. Bill even borrowed the $5,000 down payment from his credit union, to be repaid $100 a month. After all expenses, including the mortgage payment, Bill netted about $130 a month. He began to believe. He soon bought his first home for $10,000, borrowing $2,500 from the credit union for the down payment. Three years later he sold that house, using the $5,000 profit to buy a new one in Dolton, Illinois, for $24,500. One year later, in 1972, he refinanced that house for over $31,000 and used that $6,000 appreciation to buy a 3-flat priced at $30,000. He was on his way. In 1975 he used all his properties as collateral to buy a $90,000 eight-flat. In 1976, he used some of his properties as collateral to borrow $25,000 and bought four 12-flats, on contract, at $170,000 each. he later bought a 64-flat building for $500,000 and after that three houses and a condominium. He also bought 2 21-flats, a shopping mall and hundreds more till now, always managing to obtain 100% Financing for his properties, and he had the knowledge and experience to pass on to others.

One of those others was Kevin Vaughan, who began as a real estate salesman and is now a broker-owner of a realty company. Kevin knew and used all the conventional ideas for buying and selling property on behalf of his client. Although he had taught real estate classes, he decided to take Bill Joseph's seminar to expand his knowledge. He liked what he heard and, with Bill's encouragement, began investing on his own, thus proving to himself the validity of Bill's theories.

He also continued expanding his interest and influence in the real estate industry as a member of the Illinois and the National Association of Realtors, the Chicago Real Estate Board, and the South West Suburban Board of Realtors. He has served on numerous committees, such as the Professional Standards Committee, Political Involvement Committee, and Licensing Forum Committee for the Illinois Association of Realtors, and the Energy Committee for the Chicago Board. He is currently involved in sight locations for a major franchise, condominium conversions, management of properties, and in virtually all aspects of the real estate industry.

His own success persuaded Kevin to join Bill in giving the seminars so that together they could reach more people. Now Kevin also spends many hours consulting with graduates of the seminars on the purchases and the management of their properties. Together they make lectures to professional groups and host their own radio talk show, "Investing Today", with Bill Joseph and Kevin Vaughan.

The logical next step was for Bill and Kevin to put their tested and proven methods on paper for those who couldn't attend a seminar. In clear, down-to-earth language, they guide the reader every step of the way through their principles of real estate investing with the goal of financial independence.

They help you first look for and recognize a good buy. They teach you ways to create a good credit rating. Then they steer you through the steps of negotiating and financing the purchase, and provide examples of various contracts. They show you how to manage your property to increase its income, value, and eventual saleability. They explain tax and depreciation advantages and pitfalls. And for those who are interested in more complicated arrangements, they discuss trading, pyramiding, and condominium conversions among other aspects of real estate.

Everything the reader wants to know—and needs to know—is covered. And as Bill himself is the first to say: If he could do it—*you* can do it.

INTRODUCTION
How To Use This Book and Achieve Your Goals

INTRODUCTION
How To Use This Book
and Achieve Your Goals

Real estate can be the key to your dreams only if you stop dreaming and unlock the door to investing. To succeed in investing, however, you first must set definite goals. According to the Oxford Dictionary, a goal is the object of effort or ambition. The possibilities in real estate are so enormous that many people are swayed into thinking they can get something for nothing. But as good as the returns can be, they are returns for *effort*. Effort involves planning. Planning implies goals—long term goals and short term goals.

For instance, your immediate goal could be to find and purchase an apartment building worth $300,000. Your intermediate goal could be to buy one apartment building a year for the next five years. Your long term goal could be to own one million dollars in real estate in ten years. Your ultimate goal could be financial independence for the rest of your life.

Whatever your goal, this book can be your guide along the real estate investment path. But *you* have to take the first step on that path.

We suggest, as your first step: read the Preface and Table of Contents of this book to get an overview of what topics will be covered. Then read the entire book through one time to gain a general grasp of the material. (If you're an experienced real estate investor, you may want to turn immediately to those chapters that contain specific information you need, such as depreciation and taxes, contracts, or managing your property). When you have finished the book, you are ready to re-read and prepare for action.

One word of caution: you are ready to put the principles of real estate investment into action *if* your own financial house is in order. That means *credit.* You need to know what you own and what you owe! If you don't have a good credit rating, study the chapter on credit for information on creating and improving your credit situation. Your credit rating is your ticket to 100% Financing. Whether you eventually finance your purchase through a bank, directly from the seller, or other loan sources, you must always present a clean financial statement to the lender. We have included a sample financial statement in our credit chapter. Any bank will be glad to give you a copy of the one they use. Fill out the statement completely. You may be surprised.

Next, add up all your expenses and your total income for the past year. You shouldn't consider borrowing more money if you can't handle your current income and outgo.

Once your financial affairs are in order, establish a time schedule of weekly or monthly periods for real estate pursuits. Be patient and willing to invest the needed time to find the "buys"—the proper investments for your purposes. As you progress, analyze the results of your investments and be willing to re-evaluate and readjust your plans.

You might want to consider the words of Logan Pearsall Smith: There are two things to aim at in life: first, to get what you want; and, after that, to enjoy it. Only the wisest of mankind achieve the second."

Well, we won't say we're the wisest—but we can tell you three ways to retire comfortably on your real estate investments:

1. Spend about four hours a week looking for "buys" to pick up now and sell for a handsome profit when you retire. At that time, your personal income will be very low, and consequently your capital gains taxes will also be very low.

2. Live off the income from rental. We use the following rule-of-thumb: a good investor should clear approximately $50 per rental unit per month, after all expenses and payments are paid. Set a goal of owning at least 100 units so that when you retire you will clear $5,000 per month, or $60,000 per year. Depending on depreciation, you may end up with much of it tax-free.

3. Buy at least seven buildings of at least 12 units per building, during the next seven years. At the end of seven years, sell all seven buildings and become the "paper-man or paper-woman"—hold the mortgages as banks do. You (instead of the banker) will then

receive a monthly check from each of the seven new owners, and you won't have to do any work for it—no supervision or advertising ever again.

Of course, whichever retirement method and goal you choose, you must do one thing, take that first step into your future—now!

1
LEVERAGE
Or The Art of Using
Other People's Money—100%

1
LEVERAGE
Or The Art of Using
Other People's Money—100%

The art—and the heart—of making big money in real estate investing is Leverage. That's another word for borrowed money. The object is to use a little bit of money to control a very large investment. No matter how much money you have—you are better off *not* using it. Whose money do you use then? Other people's money.

Here's how.

Let's say you want to buy a $250,000 apartment complex. The seller is willing to give you a $225,000 mortgage. You go to the bank and *borrow* $25,000 against the equity in your home to use as the down payment. (Note: You have just concluded a 100% Financing deal because *all* the money for the purchase was borrowed.) If the bank charges you 16% interest you would pay $4,000 a year in interest charges. Therefore, your actual investment in the complex is $4,000 because that's the only amount coming out of your own pocket.

Now let's assume your property appreciates in value approximately ten percent—a conservative figure. (In a later chapter we show you how to control income and expenses to achieve that minimum appreciation. If you add in inflation, then an appreciation of 15% wouldn't be unusual.) This means that the $250,000 complex would increase in value $25,000 the first year, making it worth $275,000.

Now let's suppose you turned around and sold the complex, paid off the $225,000 mortgage, paid off the $25,000 bank loan, and deducted the $4,000 of interest payments. That would leave you $21,000 profit, (the increased value of $25,000 less the $4,000 interest charges). In other words, you made more than five times your initial investment—or over 500%! And in one year. And leverage did it for you. How? How does ten percent appreciation translate into 500% profit? By borrowing.

The ten percent appreciation is on the *total* value of the building complex—$250,000. But your profit is on the amount you actually invested—$4,000. A little controls a lot.

Let's take another look at the $250,000 complex. Assume you paid cash—$250,000 of your own money. Appreciation is still 10%. You sell the building a year later and pocket $25,000 profit. But that's a 10% return on your cash investment. The same $25,000—but not the same return. Or suppose you drew the $25,000 down payment from your savings account. Same building; same 10% appreciation; same $25,000 profit. Now you've made a 100% return on your cash investment. That's good. But 500% is even better. Especially when you remember that even using your own cash costs something—the interest you would have been receiving if it were still in your bank account.

Then again—suppose you don't have $25,000 cash. With 100% Financing, you at least stand to make $25,000, or 500%. That's some consolation.

Now even a 500% return doesn't make you a millionaire in one year. But the *compounding* quality of appreciation over a period of time can do that for you. (Compounding is earning appreciation on appreciation, as well as on the original amount. If you earned 10% on $100,000 the first year, you would earn 10% on $110,000 the next year, and 10% on $121,000 the year after that.)

Let's take the same apartment complex that you buy for $250,000, with a $225,000 mortgage, and a $25,000 bank loan, so you begin with *no* equity. Equity is the difference between what you owe on a property and what the property is worth. (If you own property worth $250,000 and owe $250,000, your equity is zero.) If you borrowed the $25,000 from equity of another piece of real estate you would have simply moved equity from one property to another, now owning two buildings.

Now let's see what happens when you *don't* sell the building after the first year, but hold on to it and let the 10% appreciation compound annually.

	Equity	**New Value**
After 1st year	$ 25,000	$275,000
After 5th year	152,627	402,627
After 10th year	398,435	648,435

Imagine those figures compounded at an annual rate of 15%!

Remember that you began without a penny of your own money, and a yearly interest debt of $4,000. (In a later chapter we show you how to buy and manage your property so that tenants pay off your mortgage and interest debt for you. By the way, you don't pay taxes on that yearly appreciation—in fact you save on taxes—but that's in a later chapter, too.)

But appreciation is only one part of your profits and equity. We didn't include the reduction of your mortgage debt. Depending on your mortgage agreement, the above building could be paid off in 20 years. In that case, your equity automatically jumps another $225,000—a quarter of a million dollars.

Yes, people can use leverage for other investments—like gold and stocks. But only in real estate do you have *control* over your investment—and the chance for 100% Financing. Only in real estate can you make leverage work *for* you while *you* control the risk and the profits. With the powerful tool of leverage, intelligent real estate investing can make you financially independent.

THE PRICE OF LEVERAGE: INTEREST

Leverage, as any powerful tool, must be used with skill and caution. Leverage is, after all, borrowed money; and borrowed money has its price—the interest rate charged, and the terms of repayment.

Therefore, you not only want to borrow the most amount of money—but you want the *lowest* possible interest rate with the *largest* period of time to repay.

You might say that's obvious. The theory may be obvious, but the escalation in costs over the years, and the increase in risk from overextending yourself, may not be as obvious. Yet your entire investment can be jeopardized if your monthly payments are too high—even if your purchase was a good buy! You can endanger your cash-flow, your appreciation, and lose control over your timing and sales price.

Let's see what happens when your payments become too high. For one thing, your cash-flow tends to become negative. That means you must dig into your pocket every month to cover expenses. You then may try to dig into your tenants' pockets in the form of higher rents. If your rents are too high for the area, you run the risk of unnecessary vacancies. Those vacancies mean more money out of your own pocket. Then you may find you can't afford to make necessary repairs. If you let the building run down that means lower rents eventually and lower income. That lower income lowers the value of your building. Depending on the drain on your resources, you could continue in a downward spiral all the way to a forced sale—forced either by you, the bank, or the Internal Revenue Service. So be aware that your terms of repayment are crucial to the success of your investment.

Now let's compare some actual figures: financing $300,000 at 8% interest, 12% interest, and 16% interest for the same number of years—30 years.

	8%	12%	16%
Mortgaged amount	$300,000.00	$300,000.00	$300,000.00
Monthly payment	2,202.00	3,087.00	4,035.00
5 years (60 payments)	132,120.00	185,220.00	242,200.00
30 years (360 payments)	792,720.00	1,111,320.00	1,452,600.00

Your monthly payment is about $1,800 less at 8% interest than 16%. The savings in finance charges is about $110,000 in just five years; and over $650,000 during the term of the loan. You'll pick up some savings on your interest charges, depending on your tax bracket (a later chapter deals with taxes in depth). But your main concern is your high monthly payments. They can mean the difference between your pocketing over $20,000 a year—or pulling it *out* of your pocket.

The percentage rate is only half of the leverage story. The term of the loan—how long you have to pay it back—is the other half. Now compare that $300,000 mortgage, at 10% interest, over 15 years and over 30 years.

Monthly Payments

	15 year term	30 year term
$300,000 mortgage at 10%	$3,225.00	$2,634.00

You pay $691 per month less on the longer term. That $691 allows you a greater tax flow either for expenses or to take home as profit. We're talking $8,292 a year. (Cash flow, remember, is the amount of money left over after all expenses, such as heating, electric, water, supplies, taxes, maintenance, etc. are paid, *plus* the payments of principal and interest made on the amount borrowed.) Leverage, therefore, plays a crucial role in cash flow, and ultimately in the value of your building.

Take, for example, a 12-flat apartment building priced at $250,000, on which you make a down payment of $20,000, and obtain a mortgage of $230,000 at 8% for 25 years. The annual income from rents is $40,000. The expenses, not including payments on the mortgage, are $12,500. That makes the *net income* $27,500 for one year. Now you subtract the principal and interest of $21,307 (12 payments), and end up with a cash flow of $6,193.

Annual income	$40,000
Less expenses	– 12,500
Net income	27,500
Mortgage payments	– 21,307
Cash flow	$6,193

Now watch that cash flow grow for ten years when all figures are compounded at 10% a year (just as the appreciation was), except the loan payments which remain the same.

Year	Annual Income	Annual Expense	Net Income	P&I Payment	Cash Flow
1	$40,000.00	$12,500.00	$27,500.00	$21,307.00	$6,193.00
2	44,000.00	13,750.00	30,250.00	21,307.00	8,943.00
3	48,400.00	15,125.00	33,275.00	21,307.00	11,968.00
4	53,240.00	16,637.50	36,602.50	21,307.00	15,295.50
5	58,564.00	18,301.25	40,262.75	21,307.00	18,955.75
6	64,420.40	20,131.38	44,289.03	21,307.00	22,982.03
7	70,862.44	22,144.51	48,717.93	21,307.00	27,410.93
8	77,948.68	24,358.96	53,589.72	21,307.00	32,282.72
9	85,743.55	26,794.86	58,948.69	21,307.00	37,641.69
10	94,317.91	29,474.35	64,843.56	21,307.00	43,536.56

Your expenses went up about 2½ times. But your cash flow increased seven times! That means more than just cash in your pocket. Take another look at the net income: $64,844. Remember the original net income was $27,500. Now my rule of thumb when making an offer—and when selling is *ten times the net*. For example, I wouldn't want to pay more than $275,000 for the building originally. Less, if possible—but no more. Using that same *ten times the net* rule on the new net income, means the building's value after ten years is $648,435! It has more than doubled in value, and at the same time, you are pocketing $43,536 a year from the cash flow.

Don't let the big numbers scare you. The same rules apply on small or large purchases. Leverage—borrowed money—is still the basis of a larger rate of return. Look again at the first year's cash flow of $6,193. Based on a $20,000 cash investment, that's a 31% return the first year—*not counting appreciation.*

O.K. you say. Leverage is tied to borrowing a lot of money at a low interest rate for a long time. But how do you get a lower interest rate? Ask. We go into the details in our chapters on negotiation and contracts, but essentially the best way to get a lower interest rate is to learn how to ask for it.

People tell us all the time that you can't get 8%, 9%, or 10% interest rates in the 1980's. But that's just not true. Since 1971, including 1983, I have paid 10% interest or less for the real estate I purchased. Remember that the seller probably bought the property some years ago with a lower rate of interest and for a much lower price. Therefore, you first ask the seller to finance the mortgage. Second you make a *creative offer.*

For example, a student of ours wrote in his offer (later accepted) that he would make *principal payments only* for the first year, instead of the usual principal and interest combination payment. As you know, most of the early normal payments go for interest and very little of that amount reduces the principal. Therefore, this student made 12 monthly payments of only $12 each! He explained to the seller that he needed the initial low payments so he could use the first year's cash flow to fix up the building complex.

Did you find the hidden leverage? The seller actually "loaned" the buyer the interest payments for the first year.

To sum up—if you can't buy a piece of real estate at the best interest rate for you, then don't buy it. If you extend yourself with high monthly payments, you can end up being the seller-who-has-to-sell.

Then some smart buyer is going to ask *you* for a lower interest rate, and you will probably have to give it to him!

2
TYPES OF REAL ESTATE FOR INVESTMENT

or
It's Real Estate All Right But Is It All-Right Real Estate?

2
TYPES OF REAL ESTATE FOR INVESTMENT
or
It's Real Estate All Right But Is It All-Right Real Estate?

You have a choice of different types of real estate for investment purposes. Some types provide fewer risks, some better tax shelters, and some a higher return. Every type is not right for every person, and we believe that certain types of real estate are better and safer investments than others. The different types are:

1. Land (vacant)
2. Residential
   A. Houses
   B. Condominiums
   C. Apartments (up to and including 4 units)
3. Apartment buildings (5 units or more)
4. Commercial
   A. Shopping centers
   B. Business districts—office buildings
5. Industrial—warehouses

Bear in mind that the advantages of investing in real estate rest in its four ways to make money: appreciation, cash flow, tax shelter, and equity (reduction of mortgage). And also it's leverage—borrowing power—that creates the handsome return on your investment.

LAND

Many investors have made millions investing in vacant land. They usually have succeeded because of their foresight, their determination, and their ability to persevere during rough times. The profit in vacant land comes from being able to predict the trend of growth in a given area. But too often something happens to change the course—or rate—of the predicted growth. Many factors can alter your best laid plans, such as changes in the economy; zoning and re-zoning; proposed federal expansion through highways, waterways, and housing; major business or population shifts; and even Mother Nature. In other words, you lose one of the plusses of real estate investment—control. You have no control over the predicted growth.

We're sure there are many investors who would be willing to sell, if they could, land they purchased in what was sold as good growing areas (Florida, Arizona, Arkansas, etc.).

We're not saying that land as an investment is automatically bad. We are saying that buying and selling vacant land is speculative and risky and requires careful examination. In order to invest in land you must be willing to sit it out until you receive your profit (which could take until the next generation); or take a loss. Therefore, be clear about what you are trying to accomplish with your investment.

Land as an investment has other disadvantages in comparison with other types of real estate. You cannot leverage it to the same extent. Usually, you must pay the full purchase price or put at least 50% down on a parcel of vacant land. Furthermore, you cannot depreciate vacant land, so you are denied a paper loss to shelter income. You are not receiving any cash flow—no rent. Yet you must still pay real estate taxes.

Therefore, only two of the four ways to make money from real estate apply to vacant land—appreciation and equity. But vacant land usually appreciates at a slower rate than improved property and may not keep up with inflation. You achieve some equity, but also at a lower rate—and instead of your tenants paying off your loan—*you're* paying it.

The following example compares the appreciation and equity of a piece of vacant land with those of a small house:

	Appreciation	Equity	Percentage of Profit
Land			
$20,000	8% average	$20,000	
(paid in full)	year increase	+ 1,600 appreciation	8%
	$1,600	$21,600	
House			
$60,000	10% average	$10,000 (down payment)	
($10,000 down)	year increase	+ 6,000 appreciation	60%
	$6,000	$16,000	

Your investment in land has returned you an 8% profit.

Your investment in the house has returned you a 60% profit. And that's not adding in the other advantages as noted above.

Why would anyone invest in vacant land, given this example? The only answer is that they are predicting a far greater return *eventually.* But that prediction implies a greater amount of risk. Risk and return—they usually go together. We believe, however, that other real estate investments offer a reduced risk *and* an excellent return, as you will see later in this chapter.

RESIDENTIAL

Residential real estate is composed of three types: single family house, condominium, and owner-occupied apartments of up to, and including, four units. The majority of people own one or more of these types, and many of them don't even consider themselves to be investors—especially if they live in the building and call it "home".

Many people are more comfortable with residential real estate as an investment. They feel that control is easier to maintain and the risk of investing is more limited. These two advantages come into play especially when you live in the residence. Plus you can still achieve two of the four ways to make money: appreciation and growth of equity through mortgage reduction. You achieve the other two ways to make money only if you rent the single family residence or the other apartments in a multi-unit building, because then you are adding cash-flow and the tax advantages of depreciation. You cannot depreciate your own home, or the apartment you're living in, if you live in a multi-unit building owned by you. However, you do achieve some tax advantages in the form of deductions you're allowed for interest payments on your mortgage and real estate taxes. Just how much an advantage these are depends on your tax bracket—that is, if you're in the 30% tax bracket you save 30% of these expenditures; in the 50% tax bracket you save 50%. (Tax sheltered income and depreciation are fully explained in a later chapter.)

Let's take a closer look at each type of residential real estate for investment purposes:

Single Family Home

If you bought your home for $60,000, and if appreciation is running about 10% per year, then your home's value the first year would be $66,000. (Rates of appreciation may have dropped recently, but as demand increases, so will the rate.) The second year your home appreciates $6,600 more (10% of $66,000), to $72,600. The third year your home appreciates $7,260 more (10% of $72,600) to reach $79,860. Notice that because appreciation *compounds* (you get appreciation on appreciation), your home has grown in value $19,860. Of course you are expected to maintain the property to achieve the maximum value.

If you lived in this single family home, then you not only have sheltered your family, but you have reduced your mortgage, thereby increasing your equity (the value of your home less any debt). In addition, you have garnered tax deductions in the amount of interest paid each year on your mortgage, and your real estate taxes. You have also achieved one more huge advantage that most people never use. Leverage. You can now borrow on that increased valuation. (Our chapter on financing can show you the many possible avenues for leverage.)

Now suppose you have a $50,000 mortgage at 12% interest, amortized over 25 years, resulting in a monthly payment of $526.61. (To amortize is to divide the total principal and simple interest over a fixed term). That payment includes an amount towards your interest and the balance towards reducing your principal. The payment is arrived at as follows:

$50,000
× .12   (12% interest rate)

$ 6,000   divided by 12 = $500 (the first month's interest)
Subtract that from the original monthly payment of $526.61, and you get the amount paid on principal of $26.61.

$526.61   monthly payment of principal and interest
− 500.00   first month's interest

26.61   paid on principal first month

Subtract the amount paid on principal from the principal balance of $50,000, to get your new principal balance:

$50,000.00
− 26.61

49,973.39   now owed on the mortgage

You repeat this process for the second month, using the new principal balance of $49,973.39

$49,973.39
×   .12   (12% interest rate)
$ 5,996.81   divided by 12 = $499.73 (the second
             month's interest)

    $526.61   monthly payment of principal and interest
− 499.73   second month's interest
    26.88   paid on principal second month

$49,973.39   previous balance after one month
− 26.88
49,946.51   new balance owed on mortgage

Repeat the process a total of 300 times (25 years) and you will have the amount of principal, interest payment, and mortgage balance for any given month. As you can see just from these examples (and from the following chart), very little of your monthly payment is applied toward the principal during the early years. The payment doesn't change each month—just the amounts applied toward principal and interest. As one amount becomes larger, the other becomes smaller. As the chart shows, you will be paying more toward interest for the first 20 years. At the end of 25 years you'll have paid $107,987.20 in interest alone. Adding the $50,000 mortgage payment, you will have paid a total of $157,987 in monthly payments, plus the $10,000 down payment, to make a grand total of $167,987 for your $60,000 house.

YEAR	PRINCIPAL	INTEREST
1	$ 337.48	$ 5,981.84
2	$ 380.26	$ 5,939.06
3	$ 428.52	$ 5,981.84
4	$ 482.86	$ 5,890.80
5	$ 544.09	$ 5,836.46
6	$ 613.10	$ 5,775.23
7	$ 690.84	$ 5,706.22
8	$ 778.47	$ 5,628.48
9	$ 877.21	$ 5,540.85
10	$ 988.44	$ 5,330.88
11	$ 1,113.81	$ 5,205.51
12	$ 1,225.07	$ 5,064.25
13	$ 1,414.25	$ 4,905.07
14	$ 1,593.61	$ 4,725.71
15	$ 1,795.71	$ 4,523.61
16	$ 2,023.46	$ 4,295.86
17	$ 2,280.08	$ 4,039.24
18	$ 2,569.27	$ 3,750.05
19	$ 2,895.10	$ 3,424.22
20	$ 3,262.28	$ 3,057.04
21	$ 3,676.02	$ 2,643.30
22	$ 4,142.23	$ 2,177.09
23	$ 4,667.56	$ 1,651.76
24	$ 5,259.52	$ 1,059.80
25	$ 5,930.76	$ 392.76
TOTAL	$50,000.00	$107,987.20

But part of that $107,987.20 of interest was deductible from your taxes every year. For instance, in the 10th year, if you were in the 40% tax bracket, you would save 40% of your interest costs or $2,132.35 (40% of $5,330.88). If your taxes were $2,000, you would save another $800 (40% of $2,000). In other words, Uncle Sam gave you $2,932.35 to help out with expenses.

Another way of looking at interest rates is that if you're in the 40% tax bracket, you are paying 40% less in interest. So on a 12% interest rate, you save 4.8%, and are paying an "effective" rate of 7.2%. Many investors are willing to pay higher interest rates just because of this lower effective rate in their situation. Ultimately, what you can afford still comes down to real dollars and cents, so check with a good tax lawyer and accountant before you take on any payments that might overextend you.

So far these figures apply to the person who owns and lives in a single-family home. As good as these figures look, your money is not working to its fullest. You are not deriving the benefits from cash flow (from tenants) nor a real tax shelter (depreciation). If you rented out the house, then it becomes residential income property and you make money all *four* ways.

It is dificult to rent a single-family dwelling for enough rental money to cover the costs of loan payments and maintenance. Therefore, a negative cash flow is not unusual. Another drawback is that for every month the house stands unrented, you're losing 100% of your cash flow for that month. The way we see it, renting out single-family homes is really putting all your investment eggs in one expensive basket. But there are many happy real estate investors doing just that and we can see why. They are still making money *three* ways—appreciation, equity, and depreciation—and that's not chicken-feed.

Condominiums

Condominiums are another form of single-family home gaining in popularity. One of the major factors contributing to increased condo ownership has been the affordability—they usually cost less than a single-family detached residence. Many young investors—

singles and couples—who have been priced out of the latter market buy condominiums to get started in building equity through appreciation and mortgage reduction. Retired people, too, find condominiums a more affordable and carefree retirement investment.

Again, if you live in your own condominium, you are limited to two ways of making money: appreciation and equity (reduction of mortgage). Your deductions are similar to a single-family dwelling for tax purposes: interest payments on your mortgage loan and real estate taxes.

If you rent your condominium you reap the same investment advantages and disadvantages as when you rent a single-family home. But condominium ownership, whether for your personal residence or for rental, presents additional problems of ever-increasing maintenance costs and possible restrictive bylaws in the original condominium agreement or later amendments.

While all condominium owners share in maintenance costs of the common areas, such as roof, elevators, vestibules, utility rooms, recreation facilities, these costs inevitably increase. You will, of course, also have the costs of maintaining your personal living area, except for those provisions spelled out in the original agreement. You can also have some unpleasant surprises in the form of assessments for increased expenses, special expenditures, or whatever the condominium board decides. In other words, you don't have total control over your home or investment. In fact, some condominiums have rental restrictions, either forbidding it entirely, or allowing it for short term rentals only.

In other words, before you buy a condominium for your home or investment purposes, be sure to have a knowledgeable lawyer examine all the condominium papers before you sign any dotted line.

Our reservations about single-family dwellings for investment apply to condominiums as well. A negative cash flow is a distinct possibility and a vacancy for any month means a 100% loss of income for that month. We do not recommend an investment that has you dipping into your pocket every month just to stay even. But there are investors whose personal tax bracket and situation lead them to such an investment. Before you come to such a decision you'd best check with a good tax lawyer and accountant as well as a lawyer well-versed in condominium legalities.

Multi-Family—up to 4 Units

Of all the *residential* investments available to you (as previously defined), the best continues to be the multi-family. If you live in one of the units, you not only have a place to call home, but all the other advantages of real estate investment come into play. You cannot depreciate the unit you live in, nor derive any cash flow from it, of course, but you do have those advantages on the other apartments, as well as appreciation and equity (from mortgage reduction). (Depreciation will be covered in detail in a later chapter.)

For example, suppose you purchased a 4-unit building for $150,000 and planned to live in one of the units. The entire building would appreciate at 10% per year, for a $15,000 gain the first year. Let's assume that you—and your tenants—are reducing the principal on your mortgage at the rate of $100 per month for a total of $1,200 the first year, meaning your equity from mortgage reduction is $1,200. Then, let's suppose you were able to rent the other apartments for an amount that covered *all* your expenses, including the costs of your own unit so that, in effect, you are living "rent" free. Besides that, you are gaining the tax deduction of interest and tax expenditures. The exact savings depend on your tax bracket. *And* you can depreciate the building, except for your unit and the cost of the land. (You must always deduct an amount for land, which cannot be depreciated, as explained in the depreciation chapter.) The depreciation savings would look something like the following:

$150,000	original value of building (your purchase price)
− 30,000	land value estimated at 20%
$120,000	building net value
− 30,000	cost of your unit
$ 90,000	Base on which your depreciation is figured

According to the new tax laws, you can choose straight-line depreciation over 15 years, and therefore you have a tax deduction of $6,000 ($90,000 divided by 15). That $6,000 can be deducted from any other income you may have and saves you an amount determined by your tax bracket. If you're in the 50% bracket you save $3,000; in the 33% bracket, $2,000. That is $3,000 or $2,000 in *your* pocket which would otherwise have been sent to the government.

So let's see what you have:

$15,000	appreciation of value
+ 1,200	growth in equity (reduction of debt)
+ 2,000	or more depreciation
+ 3,800	worth of rent (you have to live *somewhere*)
$22,000	*Return* on your investment in one year.

We didn't even add up your savings on interest and tax deductions because that depends on your mortgage amount, interest rate, tax bracket and cash flow. In other words, we estimated that you just broke even there: your income from rent, over your expenditures, equaled your deductions. But it's entirely possible that you could have a small negative cash flow if the income doesn't quite cover all expenses. Then that loss can be deducted from any other income. While the benefits of your investment are sound, you usually cannot expect a large cash flow on smaller properties. Maintenance, therefore, is usually done by the owner because the expense of a janitor cannot be covered by income. But when you consider that your tenants are helping you buy the building—or even paying the whole mortgage cost—then you may be willing to handle tenant complaints and maintenance yourself.

Leverage is still working for you, but obviously at a lower rate. The smaller the property, the smaller the amount of appreciation, and therefore the smaller the return. Remember the Law of Leverage: borrow the most money at the lowest interest rate for the longest period of time. It's more difficult to put this law into practice when buying residential properties because the seller usually needs all the money to reinvest in another property. For that reason most residential sellers of multi-units cannot offer contract sales or secondary financing. On the other hand, more money may be available for mortgages because there are more sources of lenders for residential property. Some lenders may require you to live on the property in order to qualify for a loan. V.A. and F.H.A. loans are available for properties up to 4 units, and carry cheaper mortgage rates than those available for larger units. (The chapter on financing covers all sources of loans and other financing in detail.)

To summarize: Of the three types of residential real estate—single-family house, condominium, multi-unit up to 4—we hope you agree with us that the multi-unit offers you the best investment opportunities. You gain all the advantages of appreciation, equity growth, cash flow and tax sheltering (depreciation). In addition, you qualify for lower interest financing and reduce your problem of 100% loss from vacancies. These plusses also mean an easier resale in the future.

But don't stop here! Larger apartment buildings may prove an even superior investment.

Apartment Buildings (5 units or more)

Not only do all four methods of making money apply to larger multi-unit buildings, but *leverage* becomes one of your biggest allies. Owners of larger properties usually don't need all their cash from the proceeds of the sale in order to reinvest in another property. Therefore, if you properly educate them, they are more open to alternate methods of financing, or "creative" financing. (The chapter on financing covers creative financing methods in detail.)

The main concern of owners of larger properties, therefore, is the reliability of the buyer—*you*. They will forego a larger down payment, and agree that the higher interest rates make bank financing less attractive for larger properties, *if* they believe you are a reliable person, with a real stake in the property, and will continue paying your monthly payments as agreed upon. You must still check your offers with an attorney and/or an accountant to make sure you are protected against laws you may not be aware of, or restrictions on the owner's original mortgage. For instance, in Texas, second mortgages are not permitted.

While leverage is a key factor in preferring larger buildings as an investment, other advantages exist as well. Most lenders won't require you to live in the larger buildings. Their size makes them more attractive for potential condominium conversions because the greater profits to be realized will attract converters.

The four methods of making money are also enhanced. The higher price paid for larger properties means, of course, a grater appreciation. On a $100,000 building a 10% appreciation is $10,000 in one year. on a million dollar building that same 10% means $100,000ı In the same year. Your equity grows in larger amounts because you are not only paying off a greater mortgage, but you have more tenents to do it for you.

Even a possitive cash flow is easier to obtain with the larger muulti-unit building. Vacations are not as big a problem; therefore the need to dig into your own pocket is reduced. If a vacancy occurs in a 12-unit building, you lose 1/12th your income for that period. In a 3-unit building, you lose one-third. The greater the cash flow also means you can usually afford a janitor or independent agent/manager to maintain the property for you and protect you from inconvenient tenant complaints and repairs. (Our management chapter goes into detail on the subject of building management.)

With proper management, you can also lower expenses and increase income. by increasing your net income, you automatically increase the value of the property. Remember the rule: buy property at 10 times the *net* income. That rules applies when selling as well. Let's assume, for instance, that you realized you could raise rents, which were low for the area, because the building needed cosmetic improvements the previous owner was unwilling to undertake. If you followed the methods outlined in our management chapter, let's say you were able to raise rents $15 a month in a 10-unit building. That would be an extra $150 per month. Over 12 months, that would increase the net income (assuming expenses remained the same),

$1,800 per year. By following the rule of thumb—ten times $1,800 is $18,000. The new value of the building—from rent increase alone—has increased $18,000. That doesn't include appreciation from equity (mortgage reduction), or appreciation from the rate of increase for real estate that year.

There are many other options, besides rent increases, to help you improve the cash flow and the value of the building beyond the inflation rate, (see our management chapter for details). In fact, most people who fail in real estate investing, do so because all they know how to do is raise rents and therefore mismanage their properties.

Another reason for seeking multi-unit buildings as an investment, is the fact that multi-unit construction has been extremely low and partly accounts for the all-time low in existing vacancies nationwide. Even as construction begins to increase, vacancies should continue to remain low because of pent-up demand and greater population needs.

Newer properties tend to have a smaller cash flow, but greater appreciation, than older properties. Most of the newer buildings will be constructed with each unit having its own heating and cooling systems, and even individual water heaters. Some states now have laws requiring such construction. These items increase the attraction of such buildings as investments because the tenants will pay their own utilities, relieving the owners of worry about utility increases. Many current owners have similarly converted their buildings. Resale of such properties also attracts more condominium converters who can then successfully market those individual apartments to prospective buyers.

Older buildings are still attractive because of their greater cash flow and opportunity as good buys. Your investment goals should determine the type of real estate purchase you ultimately make.

Furnished vs. Unfurnished

We have found furnished apartments not worth the time and effort they require. There is enough to do with normal decorating. You don't need the added work of cleaning furniture, or replacing worn or stolen furniture, or responding to a tenant's complaint that,

"I want what Mr. Smith has because I'm paying the same amount of rent."

Furnished apartments also attract people who move frequently. A person who moves furniture into an apartment usually plans to stay for awhile and is less eager to leave for the slightest reason, such as a small increase in rent. The average renter of an unfurnished apartment moves about every five years.

COMMERCIAL

Commercial real estate investments can be the best of all, if done properly. Naturally, all four methods of making money apply: appreciation, equity, cash flow, and tax sheltering (depreciation). Commercial property includes: shopping centers; strip-store centers; office buldings; medical centers; theaters; parking lots; hotels; and business properties. Additional benefits arise from owning this type of property. You usually have fewer headaches from tenants. Except for the roof, and maybe the parking lot, the tenant takes care of everything else. And you usually have longer term leases which may include cost-of-living increases, maintenance cost increases, and even a percentage of the profits (more common in shopping centers or rentals to franchises). As the landlord, you then avoid unpleasant additions in the expense column.

Most commercial leases are either gross leases, net leases, percentage leases, or variable leases.

Gross Lease

A gross lease requires the tenant to pay one monthly fee, or a fixed rate, over the term of the lease; the landlord pays for all other expenses on the property, such as: utilities, taxes, insurance, mortgage payments, etc.

Net Lease

In net leases the tenant pays the monthly rent and also pays for all or part of the property expenses. Usually the tenant pays for the utilities they use. When utilities are on common meters, the bill is prorated based on the individual square footage. Unfortunately, the tenants will then complain, saying they use little or no heat, etc. Sometimes the tenant also pays a portion of other property expenses.

There are other types of net leases, such as double net (net net) and triple net (net, net, net).

Double net leases provide for a base rental, utilities paid by tenant, plus possibly a portion of the taxes or insurance bill.

Triple net leases provide for a base rental plus all other expenses, except for repair of the roof or insurance of the building. The rent will usually cover payment of a percentage of all bills, again based on square footage, or by dividing bills by the number of commercial units of a strip store center, office building, or large mall. The bills covered could include taxes, utilities, repair and maintenance of entire unit, insurance, snow removal, water, janitorial service, sign repair and maintenance, and landscaping.

Percentage Lease

A percentage lease provides for the tenant to pay a fixed rent plus a percentage over and above that, based on the gross or net income of the tenant. This type of lease is more common with retail business property. For example, suppose the tenant pays $1,500 a month rent, and a provision in the lease states that 5% above $50,000 the tenant would owe nothing extra. But if gross income went to $75,000, then the tenant would owe an extra $1,250 (5% of $25,000). This type of lease varies greatly from tenant to tenant.

Variable Lease

A variable lease has a provision for increases in the fixed rental charge during the lease period. It is usually written as a one-year, two-year, or three-year lease with options to renew at an increased monthly rental. For instance, a two-year lease at a base rate of $1,000 a month for the first two years, could have an option to renew the lease for an additional two years at $1,500 a month. The owner gains the security of a longer term lease, and some inflation protection, while the tenant knows exactly how much rent will be required over the same period. Another variable lease could provide for a long-term lease in which rent increases are based on the changes in the cost-of-living index provided by government figures.

The drawbacks to investing in commercial real estate are major—you must know a great deal about complex financing possibilities, the impact of general and local business conditions on a particular area and its businesses, and the make-up of the area itself.

Area plays a large role in commercial real estate. It's affected by cycles in the economy and consumer spending habits. If a particular area is hard-hit through job lay-offs, you can bet that the surrounding retail industry will be equally hard-hit, and thus create a vacancy factor.

In order to assess the possibility of success for your commercial property, you must research many factors, including: traffic counts (people passing by), access to traffic thoroughfares, transportation, jobs, growth of area, residential mix, schools, facilities and services of the community (fire, police, etc.), taxes, zoning, economic make-up of the area, vacancy levels, and the economy.

Local competition also affects the success of the businesses occupying your commercial space and thereby affects your investment as well. If a new shopping center is built a few miles away, all local business can be adversely affected. Major construction of large shopping centers continued to increase in the first part of the 80's, hurting smaller centers that were already suffering from inflation.

The demand for office space was high in the beginning of the 80's and should continue, although some areas are temporarily over-built because of the faltering economy. Condominium conversions of commercial properties have achieved moderate success and show signs of increased potential and demand.

Creative financing, exchanges, and tax planning are important factors in commercial real estate investments. Mortgage money is available to investors at prime rate (the rate banks charge their best customers) or higher. Many insurance companies have funds available for such investments, especially for larger shopping centers, high-rise office complexes and medical centers.

Many investors have done well with joint ventures because of the little time needed to oversee commercial real estate. However, you should plan commercial real estate investing only after you have had experience and success with the other investments discussed. Then make sure you do your research. Get the advice of professionals. Don't be afraid to ask questions of the management company, accountant, real esate agent, and attorneys. In most cases we are talking about hefty amounts of money, so your control over your investment and your protection, is limited to the amount of hard work you first invest in careful research of the property.

INDUSTRIAL

Many successful real estate investors never get involved with industrial real estate because of its risk and complexity. The average investor usually doesn't have the knowledge and experience necessary. Corporations and insurance companies are usually involved in some sort of industrial investment which includes warehouses, factories, light & heavy industry, trucking outfits, and manufacturing plants.

Many of the same types of leases used in commercial real estate are employed with industrial real estate, and of course all four methods of making money also apply. As with commercial real estate, the investor must have experience and knowledge of these kinds of properties and do the proper research. Many properties are sold built-to-suit-the-tenant. The general economy plays a part in the success of the property, as do the plans for building an entire industrial complex or subdivision. Accessibility to major arteries, highways, shopping and sometimes rail service all have to be considered. The scarcity of mortgage money for industrial real estate usually assures the need for investors with access to a large amount of capital.

Most of the examples in our later chapters deal with multi-family residences because we believe they offer the investor the best opportunity with the least risk. But the principles remain the same. No matter which type of real estate you choose for an investment, you must be sure that you remain in control. That means you must investigate all the facts and figures that apply to a particular piece of property and to your particular situation.

3
ESTABLISHING CREDIT

or
Credit Is As Credit Used

3

ESTABLISHING CREDIT

or
Credit Is As Credit Used

While we're growing up we're taught one value repeatedly: your word is your bond—keep your promises. Credit is no more—and no less—it is a promise. It is our word that we'll repay. For really large amounts, we usually offer collateral—something we own that could be sold by the creditor for the amount owed. Often the item being bought becomes the collateral—such as a house or car.

Sometimes we make promises we can't keep. Businesses fail for lack of cash to pay their creditors. Individuals go bankrupt, or lose their homes or possessions, because they found borrowing easier than paying back. Nevertheless, our world today cannot exist without credit. Credit allows us to buy goods now and pay for them over a period of time. Many people use credit to buy television sets, boats, appliances, airline tickets, and gifts. People today are more concerned, therefore, with their credit limits than their current net worth. And with good reason. Just imagine if you had to save up first in order to buy a house, or even a car! However, credit is only a tool. You can use it to dig yourself into a hole, or to build yourself a future through carefully chosen investments. Just as you cannot save first for a house, you cannot achieve financial independence through savings either. You must use your good credit rating to enter the world of *leverage*.

Leverage means borrowing, or using, other people's money to buy property. You use the seller's money, or the bank's or some other lender's, for the down payment and/or the mortgage. You then use the renters' money to pay off the loans. Your goal is to get as close to 100% Financing as possible. Or to *owe* as much money as you can—and as much as you can pay back!

Yet suppose you have abused, lost, or never established credit. Unfortunately, many people either have had bad experiences with credit, or are just starting out, or have paid cash for everything. Some have not applied for or used credit for a number of years. One of the questions most asked in our seminars around the country deals with credit. (Some students ask these questions only in private because they're embarrassed about their credit loss. But they shouldn't be ashamed. By coming to the seminars, and not giving up, they show great courage and pride.) Most people are surprised to learn that it isn't difficult to obtain a good credit rating in a short period of time. If you follow the steps below, you should be able to establish a credit rating that will allow you to approach any banker—or lender—for necessary funds.

1. **Send for Your Credit History**

   Under the federal Fair Credit Reporting Act, you have a right to see the files that any credit bureaus may have on you. Therefore, write to your local credit bureau (see your local phone book) giving your name, Social Security number, address, age, and enclose the necessary charge—$5 or $10. (A phone call will tell you what it is.) If you have been recently denied credit by some company which looked into your credit rating, you usually may request the above information from the credit bureau with no fee. Just tell them the name of the company that you believe checked your rating and then refused your request for a loan or credit. Some cities have more than one credit bureau so be sure that you contact each of them.

2. **Review Your Personal Credit History**

   While you're waiting to hear from the credit bureau, make a list of everyone from whom you borrowed money. Include those you may still owe and those you paid back.

3. **Make Corrections of Credit History**

   Compare the list you've drawn up with the names on the credit bureau's print-out sheet. Your next step will be to correct any errors you find, especially where debts are listed that you have already paid. Many times a credit bureau will correct errors pointed out rather than go to the trouble of investigating the situation.

You also have the right to ask the bureau to put a 100-word explanation of any judgments or late payments into your file. This explanation tells whomever requests your credit report why you suffered a blemish on your rating—such as unusual medical bills or sudden loss of employment. If nothing else, the explanation shows your new creditors that you do care about your rating.

4. **Request Payment Reports**

You may discover that some lenders have *not* reported your payments to the credit bureau. You must then draft a form letter asking them to please do so. You may also phone or visit these creditors in order to ask them personally to report your credit payments. After you allow enough time for them to comply, follow up with another request to the credit bureau for a report to see if they actually did so. These lenders, who don't always bother to report satisfactory credit behavior, could include automobile dealers, department stores, banks, and national credit card companies.

5. **Clear Report of Late Payments**

If your credit report shows any judgments or late payments that have since been cleared up, ask those creditors for a written release stating that the matter has been settled. Take that release personally to the credit bureau and ask them to remove the offending material.

6. **Negotiate Unpaid Bills**

If you have some unpaid bills that you still cannot repay in their entirety, try to negotiate the balance owed and get a release from that creditor. For example, you may owe a creditor $1,000. If you can afford only $600, ask your creditor if he will settle for that amount. Often the creditor may feel it's better to get something than nothing and will agree to give you a letter of release upon payment. For safety's sake, do not pay the amount until the release is signed.

7. **Bankruptcy**

   If you've had to file bankruptcy, your creditor can keep that report on file for seven years and then renew it. (First check your local and state bankruptcy laws with a lawyer). Again try to pay an agreed upon sum to your creditors and get your releases.

   If you've filed Chapter 13, try to repay your debts over a period of time. Make sure you keep your payments punctual.

8. **Create a Credit Rating—Pledged Account**

   If you are just getting started, or rebuilding your credit, the best and quickest method is through a pledged (secured) account. That simply means you open a savings account in a bank and then borrow it back.

   For instance, let's say you put $1,000 in a bank savings account. You then take your passbook to the loan department and borrow $1,000, using your savings account as security. Don't fear rejection because the bank has nothing to fear either. They've got your savings account to grab if you should forget to pay back the loan. Therefore, they will charge you an interest rate only a couple of percentage points over the interest they're paying you on your savings account. (If you opened a 5½% savings account, they'll probably charge you 7½% for the loan.) Those interest payments are tax deductible, just as the interest payments you receive are taxable.

   But you aren't finished yet. Now take that $1,000 you just borrowed and deposit it in another bank. And borrow it back again. And take it to another bank. And repeat the procedure all over again. And follow two rules: Be sure to make all your payments on time—or better yet, ahead of time; and add up the interest payments to make sure you can afford to pay off the loans. For instance: If you borrowed $1,000 as above, paying 8% and receiving 6%, you are actually paying out 2%—or $20 per year for each $1,000 borrowed. If you have followed this procedure at five banks, you must be sure you can repay that $100 by the end of the year. Don't accidentally spend the $1,000, either. Leave it in the last bank, unborrowed, to draw on when you begin repayments.

After some months have passed, get a new statement from your credit bureau to make sure the banks have reported your credit transactions. The final result should be an improved credit rating and several banking contacts who may lend you money in the future for your real estate investments. After all—you've just proved you're a good credit risk. And once you prove, through the above steps, that you are a good risk, you may be able to borrow several thousands of dollars "unsecured"—using just your signature. That's just another way of saying your word (name) is as good as your bond.

4
LOOKING FOR BUYS
A Step-By-Step Approach

4
LOOKING FOR BUYS
A Step-By-Step Approach

We're going to assume that most readers are serious, potential investors in real estate. But many of you are too busy trying to make a living to invest your most precious and profitable resource—TIME! Sure, you think it'd be great to use 100% Financing at low interest rates on good real estate buys. And just as soon as a good deal finds you, you'll take it.

Well, we're going to show all you people with no time to spare that it doesn't take a great deal of time to find the best buys in real estate—*if* you know what you're doing, and then do it in an organized way.

WHAT TO LOOK FOR

To start with, you're looking for properties that sell for ten times the net income. (The next chapter describes in detail how to figure, from the financial statement, whether a particular piece of property is a good buy or not.) Many such properties are termed Ugly Ducklings to imply that their defects should be merely cosmetic. You're also trying to find a seller who is willing to finance his/her property at a low interest rate. Your chances of finding the best buys and most cooperative sellers are usually related to the economic level (or income) of the population. For ease of discussion, we divide them into: upper (price), middle (price), and lower (price). Each type must be examined in relation to the four ways to make money in real estate: appreciation, depreciation, (tax advantages), equity (mortgage reduction), and cash flow. Your goal is to find a property that offers you all of these advantages. Let's look at these types one at a time.

Upper Level

People who own property in upper areas, where prices and rents are high, usually rely on appreciation and depreciation to make money. They're willing to accept a negative cash flow (sinful words) because their property is located in a very good economic area and will appreciate more, proportionately, than property in lesser areas over a period of time. The owners also bask in pride of ownership, an important component for most investors.

If you buy property in upper areas, you'll have to do what the previous owner did—wait. Wait for appreciation to raise the value of your property. Wait until rents go up, and hope they rise faster than expenses. You'll probably have to put a larger sum of money down in order to break even, or keep the negative cash flow small.

Now let's look at the *four* ways to make money: You'd have the benefit of appreciation and depreciation (but you'd have that on any income property). You would also have equity (the 30% you probably put down, plus the amount of the mortgage you're paying off). The disadvantages are: you have a negative cash flow and/or a large down payment to keep that negative cash flow small. That large down payment also reduces your leverage—and therefore your return on your investment. We prefer to use the maximum amount of leverage when we purchase real estate so that our equity doesn't just sit there. Or to put it another way, we don't want to sit on our assets.

Another major drawback of upperclass property as an investment involves the attitudes of the owner-seller. He is rarely a must-seller and therefore is less flexible when price and/or financing are negotiated. He probably accepted a negative cash flow when he bought the building and will be unsympathetic to any buyer who is trying to get terms that will create a positive cash flow. In addition, the owner of a higher-price building is often in a better position to afford a vacancy, having already allowed for a negative cash flow, and therefore less anxious about a sale.

For all of the above reasons—negative cash flow, large deposit, seller unwilling to negotiate financing—we spend little time looking for a buy among upper, or higher priced properties.

Lower Level - *Bad*

Lower priced areas are even less desirable when searching for a good buy. They don't appreciate in value as fast as other properties. Because they are less desirable, their owners don't spend much on keeping them in good condition, thus they are likely to be in great need of repair. While they'll usually have a positive cash flow, they also have a load of potential headaches. Even if you spent money on cosmetic improvements in order to justify higher rents, you'd have to wait until the whole area improved before you could get those rents.

So of the four ways to make money in real estate, you could count on only one: the cash flow—*if* you could collect the rents, and *if* expenses and repairs didn't run too high. The owner very likely would be a must-seller and flexible about negotiations—but *you* probably would become a must-seller very soon after you became the new owner.

Middle Level

We suggest, in light of the above, that you spend most of your time looking for buys in middle-price areas. These could be viewed as steppingstone areas where the owners have starter-homes, priced in the middle range, and dream of buying mansions, or better homes, some day. In the meantime, income properties in these areas appreciate nicely in value (although perhaps not as much as in the upper areas). You are more likely to uncover a must-seller who will be willing to negotiate terms with you so that you can gain a positive cash flow. Your equity will be building through your down payment, mortgage reduction, and appreciation.

You will also find a greater number of properties available in the middle area so that you can have a choice of good buys, and still achieve all four ways of making money.

Even these find properties don't come walking up to you announcing: Here I am, 100% Financing and low interest rates, with great appreciation, and a super cash flow. If they did, you probably wouldn't believe them anyway. The very fact that you have to do some work on your own is actually an advantage when investing in real estate. When you do finally uncover a good buy, you'll know it.

You'll have all those not-so-good buys and darn-they-got-away good buys to compare yours with.

WHERE TO START

The next question is *where* do you start looking. We suggest that most people start to look for buys right in their own backyard. The main reason is knowledge. The more you know about a particular area the better choices you'll make. The secondary reason is convenience. By starting in your own hometown, or business section, you save the time that you would otherwise have to spend traveling to and researching an area you don't know at all.

For instance, if you live or work in a particular town, you'll probably know that the village just passed strict fire codes, or a moratorium on condominium conversions. Had you not known what was going on, and purchased a building that was adversely affected by those changes, you could have lost money on your investment.

Living or working in an area means that you probably know your city's main source of jobs is a company or industry that is planning huge layoffs. The resulting economic fallout could mean more rental vacancies, or a loss in value of a building near that company.

When considering an area for investment possibilities, many factors have to be considered, such as traffic and population patterns (discussed later in the chapter). Some of these factors you already know about if you live in the area. Others you'll have to investigate before making a final decision.

The easiest way to find out more about an area, whether you live there or not, is to use tools such as the local newspaper, library, and city hall or village board.

Regularly scan the local newspaper for any items that could affect real estate values, such as the effect of the economy on local industry. Not so long ago it used to be a rule of thumb that the best properties were located near industry. The theory was that people want to live near their jobs. But the recession and unemployment came along and hurt those owners who had stretched their resources to the limit and could not handle a vacancy problem. Real estate investors learned that you shouldn't depend entirely on one factor alone when purchasing property. The local library may have a copy of the census that can show how your area compares in popularity with others nearby. Is it losing population, or gaining in average income per resident? If the number of households (not necessarily individuals) is increasing, that could signal a need for more housing, including rentals.

Visit the village board to find out about any requirements that might affect your ownership of property in the area. Check out the zoning maps in the City or Village Hall. They will show which areas of the city are zoned for each type of property—such as multi-family, residential commercial, industrial, agricultural, and institutional (school district). If you were planning to buy a building today in a quiet, largely undeveloped area, the maps will tell you who your neighbors will be in the future—such as a shopping center. You can also determine current and future commercial competition from these maps, and the potential supply and demand in real estate.

While you're there, ask about the tax base. Areas with a lot of factories, businesses and other commercial activity usually have a lower tax base than largely residential areas.

Are schools closing or new ones opening? The school board can tell you their projections, which also affect the demand for housing.

Are good recreational facilities provided or planned and where are they located? A park can be a plus for some locations; a band shell a minus if it means noise and heavy traffic.

Don't be overwhelmed by the thought of collecting all this information. If you've chosen to begin looking in your own backyard, as we suggested, you probably know many of the answers already. You also can postpone much of the above investigation until you've actually found your good buy. One thing for sure—it is easier and less costly to review the area *before* investing in it. The only surprise you should ever have is how quickly your property appreciates.

HOW TO SEARCH FROM YOUR OWN HOME

You can do most of the work right in the comfort of your own home. All you need to start is a phone, a pad of scratch paper, and your local newspaper.

The name of the game is *information,* and the rule is: Get more information than you give!

You're seeking four kinds of information:

1. Financial—the asking price; gross income; expenses; the net income; the type of financing
2. Psychological—why is the owner selling (a must-seller?)
3. Physical—location and condition of property
4. Comparables—what do similar properties sell for

The information sheet below ensures that you don't overlook any facts and organizes the material for you. Make up a separate sheet for each property you investigate. The information is divided into: income and expenses information; building facts; seller's reasons; financing information, and comparables.

BUILDING FACTS

1. Age of the building? _____

2. Its condition? _____

_____

3. Age of any improvements, such as a new roof, water heater, electrical, heating, or cooling systems?

_____

_____

_____

_____

4. Are the appliances owner-owned? Which ones? Who is responsible for their repair and replacement?

_____

_____

_____

5. Are the units individually heated? _____

6. Do tenants pay for their own utilities? _____
   (Heat and utility costs represent a major portion of expenses strongly affected by inflation).

SELLER MOTIVATION

One of the most important questions you can ask is: Why? Why is he selling the property? Look for someone who *must sell* his real estate. *You* need a must-seller for two reasons:

1. If you know *why* someone is selling, you can usually give them what they really want—not always the same as what they first *say* they want.

2. Then you get what *you* want, which is a good purchase price, a low interest rate, and close to 100% Financing.

A must-seller is someone who must sell for any of the following reasons:

CHECK-LIST
☐ Divorce
☐ Health
☐ Job transfer
☐ Estate settlement
☐ Owns two homes
☐ Mismanagement
☐ Bad debts
☐ Loss of tax shelter advantage (depreciation used up)
☐ Business losses
☐ Personal or family problems
☐ Retirement
☐ Tired of owner-responsibility
☐ Made a bad buy originally (paid too much, at too high an interest, with too great a negative cash flow)

As you can imagine, many people will fall into one of the above categories. You'll also find out what we found out: most people don't fail in real estate. Rather they fail, or hit snags in other areas of their lives and need their real estate to bail them out. They are further proof that real estate is one of your best investments—no matter what else you do.

FINANCING INFORMATION

1. Where is the mortgage? What is a rough estimate of balance on mortgage?

_____

_____

2. Is there a second mortgage on property? _____

3. What interest rates does seller have on any mortgages?

_____

4. Can current financing be assumed? Is it V.A. or F.H.A.? (They are assumable.)

_____

_____

5. Is owner interested in holding a second mortgage, or any type of owner financing?

_____

_____

6. Does the seller have a due-on-sale provision in his mortgage? ____

COMPARABLES—FROM REAL ESTATE AGENTS

When you buy a car, it helps to know what cars in general are selling for. Then, if you decide on an economy 2-door, you usually find out what other economy 2-doors are selling for. Investing in real estate properties works much the same way. You need to know what various types of properties are selling for in the area in which you're searching. Your main source for this information will be real estate agents. Call an agent or two and ask them how much certain types of properties are selling for in certain areas. Next, ask them to send you, or offer to stop by for, comparables—called "comps." These are sheets, or booklets, that give information on similar types of properties that have sold in the area under concern. The agents should have records of properties that have sold through their office. If they belong to a Multiple Listing Service (MLS), then they have records for all listings and sales in an area.

If you're looking for a 6-unit building, for example, you need to know what 6-unit buildings have sold for in the area, similar to the one you're seeking to buy. In other words you have to make proper comparisons—hence "comps".

Try to compare properties as similar as possible. Not all 6-unit buildings are the same. One might have six 5-room 2 bedroom units, while another might have three 5-room, 2 bedroom units, and three 4-room, 1 bedroom units. If exact comparables aren't available, then check out larger properties with similar room sizes and divisions and average them out to a cost per unit, and then compare the result with your building.

Compare the following factors:

- Size of property—6 units with 6 units (as above)

- Type of construction—brick with brick

- Size of units—5 rooms, 2 bedrooms, baths, dining rooms, garages, balconies, etc.

- Income, expenses on those sold, and those for sale

- Price—original asking price—sold price

- Timing—how long was it on the market; was it a buyer's or seller's market; what were the interest rates at various lending institutions

Value and Expenses

You can learn even more from comparables. One way to figure the average appreciation rate in your area is to check the prices that properties sold for three years earlier and what they, or similar ones, are selling for now. Also figure out the average increase in income and expenses. By noting low income and high expenses, you might discover who mismanaged their properties and were therefore forced to sell at a lower price.

But don't base your purchase solely on comps. Their main use is to determine that you aren't overpaying for your property. You must understand that ego plays a role in the pricing of properties. Everyone has pride of ownership. So let's say that you heard your neighbor down the street just sold his 6-unit for $150,000. Your building is the same model (design). But you know (ego) that your property is worth more. And it may be! But assume for the moment that they are virtually the same and you heard that your neighbor got $150,000 for his shack. You decide to place your 6-unit castle on the market for at least $185,000. If someone comes along and pays you around $185,000, all the other properties will now be worth more, according to their owners. If yours doesn't sell, even though it receives a number of showings, you wonder why. Chances are that the real estate agents are using your property to help sell all the other similar 6-unit buildings that aren't over-priced. They'll show yours and say, "Gee, you can buy another 6-unit for much less than this one." The other owners will thank you for helping them sell their properties at "lower" prices.

Hearsay should never be used as comps. Anyone who tells you a building sold for a certain price should be able and willing to show you proof. And even if it did, how do you know that the people who purchased the property didn't overpay for it? The point is that asking prices and sold prices are not necessarily true indicators of value. Comps help—but they aren't the whole thing. You still need to know as much as you can about an area, its properties for sale and sold, and to drive by to make notes on your comps, and finally to be aware of the current market. The best way to judge value is on the return—the figures.

You might think you have a lot of information to request over the phone—and you're right. You do. But you're trying to limit the amount of time spent locating your buys and the information you gather will eliminate many properties for investment. Remember that even the answers you get are just the initial information you need. You haven't even seen the property yet.

In order to set the mood that will encourage the sellers and agents to give you information over the phone, be lavish with compliments, especially to a For-Sale-By-Owner (FSBO). Let the person know what caught your attention in the ad—the location, the size of the apartments, the excellent condition mentioned. Be pleasant. Don't sound as if you're well-informed about real estate. You will either turn them off or hurt your negotiations at a later stage when they may suspect you of being the "city slicker" who is trying to "steal" their precious property.

SOURCES

You have four main sources of information:

1. Newspaper ads
2. Real estate agencies
3. Personal inspection of an area and property
4. Word-of-mouth

Now you are ready to start phoning one of the sources of information:

Newspaper Ads

First turn to the real estate classified section in your local paper and underline *all* the ads that appeal to you. Include those listed FSBO as well as those advertised by real estate agencies. You're going to phone every number you have underlined.

Newspapers also advertise estate sales, joint ventures, HUD sales (Housing and Urban Development), auctions, and persons interested in an exchange.

Naturally, the more time you put in, and the more sources you investigate, the greater your chances of finding a buy.

You can also place an ad yourself—especially if good buys sell quickly in your area, or are harder to find. You may uncover a must-seller who just hadn't gotten around to advertising. The following ad may turn up the answer to your dreams:

> Interested investor seeking small income property outside downtown area, price & terms flexible. Willing to pay top dollar if property qualifies. Contact Mr. Citizen at

312/111-0000 or mail info., to P.O. Box
000, Chicago, IL.

Real Estate Agents

Once you have been educated by an agent or two, and studied some comps, you are ready to call at least twenty ads by other agents. You will call so many because agents with really good properties might not bother to call you back with information. They will try to qualify you over the phone to try and find out how much money you actually have to work with.

Your best answer, now that you know your stuff, is, "Oh, I figure I can afford up to X amount of dollars for that 6-flat or 12-flat." Please don't tell them you're looking for 100% financed properties at low interest rates or your name will be filed under G for garbage can. Real estate agents would much rather present an all-cash offer to their clients. Your job is to find out what the seller wants so you know how to shape your offer.

Try to find some real estate offices that don't belong to a MLS because MLS members usually have the same properties to sell. (The selling tips chapter explains in detail the workings of a real estate agency). Ask the agents to mail the financial breakdown sheet (liar sheet) to your home or post office box. (Many investors prefer not to give out their home addresses.)

Once you receive their material, and if the numbers look good, drive by the property. Then let the agent know that you received the sheet and tell him or her whether you're interested in the property or not. Your prompt response proves your sincerity and makes it more likely that the agent will try to find you buys in the future.

HOW TO SEARCH BY CAR OR FOOT

One of the best ways to find apartment buys in real estate is to drive around your area. You not only can check out properties known to be for sale, but you can keep an eye out for signs of potential must-sellers. Buildings that look run-down and in need of cosmetic improvements suggest that the owner may be tired of owning and maintaining them. Signs of an uninterested owner include unkept lawns, broken windows, garbage about the property, peeling paint, and a number of vacant apartments. If the property looks on its way to being an eyesore, the owner has probably received complaints from neighbors and city inspectors. Under these conditions, you could be the first one to approach the owner before he lists his property for sale. Aggressive real estate agents obtain their listings by such means.

Knock on Any Door

If you scout your area regularly, you probably will find at least one property that fits the above description. Your next step is to locate the owner. Usually someone doing yardwork or a little repair is the owner. If he is, ask if the property is for sale. Most times he will say "sure, if the price is right."

Then all you have to do is ask for a meeting to go over his financial statement (liar sheet) for the property. To get the ball rolling, exchange names and phone numbers and set a meeting date, giving him time to get the information together for you. If he's not interested in selling, leave your name and number just in case he changes his mind. You might add that should he know of anyone else interested in selling, to let you know. This approach reinforces your message that you are really looking for property.

If the person tending the property turns out not to be the owner, it's best to pose as a prospective renter and ask if he can put you in touch with the owner or manager. Most sellers, even those who have their property listed with a real esate firm, don't want the tenants to know the property is for sale. They give strict showing instructions to their agents to insure word doesn't leak out ahead of time. You don't want to create ill feeling either with tenants or owner—before you even find out if the property might be for sale.

If no one is around, overcome your fears and knock on a door. Ask who and where the owner or manager is as above. (With smaller buildings, especially, the owners probably live in one of the apartments.) As a last resort, check the tax records at City Hall or the County Recorder's Office to find the name and address where the tax bill is sent.

Sometimes you will see on a building signs that bear the name of a management company. Such signs are meant to attract prospective tenants who may be driving around the area looking for a place to live.

Kevin called one such company and discovered that they owned all the properties in a certain area. They asked how many buildings he would be interested in! Not a bad way to find several buys at one time. Don't be put off by the size of a building, either. Remember, the bigger the property, the better the owners can afford to work with you.

While driving around the area that interests you, notice the traffic patterns and transportation facilities. Be aware of entrances and exits to local main-arterial streets. Property that is not near shopping, transportation, or schools is usually less desirable than locations that are easily accessible. Less convenient locations are harder to rent and usually command lower rentals.

If you're considering an investment in commercial real estate, assess the types of businesses and the amount of business they do. Do they draw support from local people only or from more distant areas as well? Check out the shopping centers. Are they backed or anchored by a large company such as Sears, Wards, Marshall Fields, etc.? How well are the other stores doing? Do they handle expensive, moderate, or cut-rate merchandise? How long has the center been in business? How accessible is it by car? Is there adequate public transportation to and from the center?

When you are zeroing in on a particular piece of property, take an even closer look at its general area. What is the economic make-up of the area in terms of jobs and competition? Are there hazardous plants nearby, noise problems? Is new construction planned, or expansion?

FACTORS TO CONSIDER

As you can see, the more you find out about an area, the better prepared you will be and the more problems you will avoid. Before making a final decision, do consider the following factors:

1. Industry (jobs)

2. Transportation

3. Shopping

4. Schools

5. Business base (tax revenue)

6. Competition

7. Appreciation potential (supply and demand)

8. Recreation

9. Economic level

WORD-OF-MOUTH

Whenever possible, get out and talk to people. Neighborhood people usually know when an owner is going to turn into a must-seller and can alert you before any ads or signs appear. Commercial tenants and store owners may know when their landlords are planning to sell.

Besides neighborhood people, tell professional people that you're looking for a real estate investment and that you'd appreciate hearing of any building that looks good and may be coming up for sale. Your banker is a source for any foreclosures he may come across. Your attorney can tell you about any deals that looked good but have fallen through for reasons that may not apply to you. Accountants often advise clients to shed properties that are no longer useful as tax shelters because of used-up depreciation. They can tell *you* at the same time they tell their clients.

Eventually you should build up a network of contacts who will know that you are serious about buying real estate.

THE BOLD WAY OF BUYING REAL ESTATE

You might want to try the "Bold Way" (or "Buckshot") to buy real estate. Arm yourself with 20 to 50 real estate contracts that you have prepared with several "out" clauses (explained in the chapter on contracts), and with blanks for names and addresses.

Then walk into one of the larger real estate offices and open their multiple-listing book. Start filling in names and addresses onto your 20 to 50 real estate contracts. Then hand the contracts, with promissory notes for down payments due at the date of closing, to the real estate broker.

Don't worry about all your contracts being accepted because you are going to:

1. Cut the asking price 25% to 30%.

For instance, on a $100,000 property you will offer $70,000.

2. Include the following "out clauses." (A way out for you.)

A. Purchaser has the right to see and approve the interior and exterior of building before this offer becomes final. If purchaser does not wish to continue with purchase, he will notify real estate agent:

Name_____

Company _____

within 7 days after acceptance of this offer.

B. Seller must prove that all expenses are accurate within $100 of listing sheet. If not accurate, or if the expenses are higher than informed, purchaser is not bound by this contract.

C. This offer is subject to purchaser's attorney's approval and is not binding without it. Purchaser's attorney will issue letters of approval seven days after acceptance by seller. If purchaser's attorney does not approve of contract for any reason whatsoever, seller or real estate sales person will be so notified in seven days after acceptance by seller of this contract.

After submitting all these offers, you'll be lucky to have three accepted out of 50. But, if you did find 3 must-sellers you probably found 1 to 3 terrific buys in a short period of time. As you will discover, most first offers are not accepted, probably to most buyers' relief.

But suppose you had followed the suggestion of a real estate agent to make one offer of $98,000 on a beautiful $100,000 property.

Then suppose the seller accepted the contract terms right away. You would probably walk through life scratching your head and asking yourself how much less you could have bought it for.

That might be reason enough to try the Buckshot method—if you feel bold enough. We tell our students that if they spend about four hours a week looking for buys, and if they find just one a year for the next four to seven years, they would have a substantial net worth and not have to worry about money in future years. Remember that each time you buy one building, you can use it as collateral for the next one. (You must either have the deed or find someone willing to accept an A.B.I. Assignment of Beneficial Interest, as explained in the financing chapter.) Just imagine how inflation and appreciation can work for you when you own several buildings at the same time.

Is a future free from financial worry worth four hours a week? The people who invest in real estate think so.

BUYING YOUR OWN RESIDENCE

Use the same techniques for finding a good buy when buying your own home as you do when buying investment property. A local real estate office has listings of homes that will give you an idea of the price range and the availability of certain types of homes in certain locations. If you look at twenty homes and select one, you should do better than if you look at two and pick one. In the matter of your own home, of course, personal preferences will color your choice.

This is definitely a buyer's market as many sellers are in a distress situation because of the high cost of living, moving, high interest rates, and perhaps loss of a job. Ideally you buy in a buyer's market and sell in a seller's market. But even if you have very little money, you're still in a buyer's market when you find a must-seller.

5
ZEROING IN
Selecting Your Buy

5
ZEROING IN
Selecting Your Buy

By now you have done your homework and found a number of potentially good buys. How do you decide which building is the best investment? The key is the financial statement (liar sheet) which should save you much running around and further investigation.

Remember the oldie: figures don't lie, but figurers do. Therefore, you must first verify expenses. Of course, don't ask for verification of expenses, copies of leases, etc. unless you are serious about that building as an investment. And in order to be serious, that building must be priced at or around ten times the net income, and/or you have a feeling the owner is willing to negotiate—a must-seller.

The financial statement on any building should include the same information as you asked for in chapter four (Looking for Buys). If necessary, get the owner's account number on the utility bills so you can call or write the companies. They will usually send you copies of the actual bills charged to that building. On most liar sheets you will get outdated expenses or projected rents—not the current figures. Often the owner will start to raise rents in the building just prior to selling. He may try to base his price on a few new leases. Before that, the rents were probably low for the area. You need the leases in order to determine a breakdown of all rents, security deposits, how large each unit is (number of bedrooms, baths), and which units are occupied by whom. All these figures and information should help you to decide how you can raise income and lower expenses.

If the owner won't divulge any information prior to a written offer, you simply make your offer subject to verification of those items (see our contracts chapter). It's very important to check all information prior to closing. Many people have been burned by "hot" properties because they didn't do their investigative work beforehand. Don't fall in love with the building *or* the tenants. Determine the best buy on paper out of all the possible purchases. Later chapters will discuss writing the offer and negotiating the terms to get the best buy possible.

Let's look at six different income and expense sheets on six pieces of property, each with six units to rent—and try to select the best buy from these figures alone. (It's more difficult to meet the ten times the net income rule on buildings with fewer than 4-6 units.)

You should also have (from real estate agents) copies of comps (comparable properties) that have sold so you can compare expenses and rents from property to property, area to area. By comparing those that have sold in the past to those currently for sale, you can also figure out the percentage rate of increases in taxes, utilities, income, etc.

Building A

1. Type of building	6-unit apartment building
2. Asking price	$150,000
3. Annual gross income	18,000

Average monthly rent: $250
Average rent in area: $270

4. Annual expenses	8,150
Taxes	$2,500
Caretaker	600
Gas	1,000
Electric	400
Water	400
Waste disposal	300
Supplies	700
Maintenance	200
Miscellaneous	50
Insurance	2,000
	$8,150

5. *Annual net income $ 9,850

*Gross income less expenses—not including any mortgage payments.

Going by our rule—10 times net income—we don't want this one unless we can purchase it for about $98,500. Even if the rents were $270, the asking price is still too high.

Building B

1. Type of building	6-unit apartment building
2. Asking price	$125,000
3. Annual gross income	17,500

    *Average monthly rent: $243 same in area.

4. Annual expenses:		$ 3,800
Taxes	$1,400	
Caretaker	0	
*Gas	0	
*Electric	0	
Water	400	
Waste disposal	325	
Supplies	350	
Maintenance	225	
Miscellaneous	100	
Insurance	1,000	
	$3,800	

5. Annual net income $ 13,700

    *Note: This is an all electric building—tenants pay electricity.

This one seems to fit our mathematical requirements. We must figure in an expense for a caretaker, however, because we don't wish to do the work. Estimating a caretaker at $700 a year the building would still net $13,000 annually, placing the approximate value at $130,000. We will drive out and look at this one.

Building C

1. Type of building   6 stores
2. Asking price $200,000
3. Annual income   21,600
   Average monthly rent: $300
4. Annual expenses*   0
5. Annual net income $ 21,600

*Note: The leases require the tenants to pay for all expenses as is customary in retail establishments.

This commercial property seems like a good purchase because the income should make it pay for itself. The leases are not unusual for such a property and at ten times the net income, the building would be valued at $216,000. Worth a look.

Building D

1. Type of building   6-unit apartment building
2. Asking price $220,000
3. Annual income   25,200
   Average monthly rent: $350
   same as area.
4. Annual expenses $ 10,200
   Taxes $4,200
   Caretaker   800
   Gas   1,200
   Electric   400
   Water   450
   Waste disposal   350
   Supplies   450
   Maintenance   250
   Miscellaneous   100
   Insurance   2,000
                      $10,200
5. Annual net income $ 15,000

Even though the rents are higher in this building, the net income is not large enough to support the asking price. With the average rent in the area the same, you have no chance of increasing income in the near future. We would not recommend an investment of this type. When money is tight, such as during a recession, it is harder to rent more expensive apartments. With such high expenses, and if you paid near that asking price, a few vacancies could bury you—and you would become a must-seller.

Building E

1. Type of building   6-unit apartment building
2. Asking price $165,000
3. Annual gross income   19,080
   Average monthly rent: $265
   same in area.
4. Annual expenses $ 2,250

Gas	$1,000
Electric	400
Water	450
Waste disposal	300
Supplies	100
	$2,250

5. Annual net income $ 16,830

Even though the net annual income supports the asking price, we would not want this building. The seller is not telling all. He omitted the expenses of taxes, insurance, and caretaker maintenance. The amount allotted for supplies is ridiculously low. This financial statement is an example of what we call the liar sheet. To protect yourself against false figures, ask the seller or real estate agent for a copy of the bills and proof of income by means of copies of the leases. If the owner has nothing to hide, he will give them to you. If he will not release such information until he receives an offer, make sure that your lawyer is aware that you want proof of all expenses and the figures are subject to your approval.

Building F

1. Type of building		6-unit apartment building
2. Asking price		$150,000
3. Annual gross income		18,000

Average monthly rent: $250
Average area rent: $270

4. Annual expenses		$ 8,800
Taxes	$3,100	
Caretaker	600	
Gas	550	
Electric	450	
Water	600	
Waste disposal	400	
Supplies	500	
Maintenance	450	
Miscellaneous	150	
Insurance	2,000	
	8,800	
5. Annual net income		$ 9,200

Again, the net income doesn't support the asking price. Even if the rent were raised $20 per month per apartment, the net income would increase only $1,440 a year, for a total of $10,640—still not justifying the asking price. The amount listed for gas is very low for a

6-unit building. You'd best proceed with caution, asking for proof of expenditures, as in building E.

Instead of bemoaning the amount of effort involved, look at it another way. The more buildings you look at, the more familiar you will become with income and expenses.

GROSS ANNUAL INCOME MULTIPLIER

Some appraisers use the gross annual income method to figure value. If the building was collecting $30,000 a year in rent, and the multiplier in that particular area was 10, then the building would be appraised at $300,000 (10 × the gross annual income). The multiplier changes for different areas and sometimes from appraiser to appraiser.

The following example shows how real estate properties are valued by the multiplier of gross annual income:

Type of Area	Gross Annual Inc.	Multiplier	Value of R.E.
Bad area	$30,000	2	$ 60,000
Good area	$30,000	10	$300,000
Excellent area	$30,000	12	$360,000
Best area	$30,000	14	$420,000

We do not like this method of appraising value. We prefer the net income method because two buildings can have the same annual gross incomes, but differ hugely on the net annual income, depending on which is run most efficiently.

Compare the following two 12-unit apartment buildings:

	A	B
Annual Gross Income	$30,000	$30,000
Expenses:		
Taxes	4,000	5,000
Caretaker	600	1,200
Gas	0*	2,300
Electric	0*	700
Water	400	500
Waste disposal	350	400
Supplies	200	650
Maintenance	300	1,000
Miscellaneous	150	200
Insurance	2,500	3,000
Total Expenses	8,500	14,950
Net annual income:	$21,500	$15,050

*Tenants pay

In the example you will note that both have the same gross annual incomes. The expenses in building A are at least $6,000 *less* than in building B. That is $6,000 to use on your loan payment or put in your pocket. Assuming the expenses are verified, there is no way we would pay the same price for both buildings.

The size of the building or number of apartments does not change the rule of 10 times the net income. Whether the building is for sale at $100,000 or a million dollars, the small numbers tell the story. Following is a 40-unit rental building:

# of Rentals	# of Rms. per Unit	Description	Rent per Unit	Total Mo. Income
5	Efficiency	Unfurnished	$235	$1,175
15	1 B.R.	"	$270	$4,050
20	2 B.R.	"	$305	$6,100
40 units	Gross annual income			$135,900
	Total annual expenses			− 35,900
			Net income	$100,000

We would not pay more than $1,000,000 for this property.

Let's take the figuring one step farther—to cash flow. To remind you, cash flow is the amount of money left *after* all operating expenses are deducted from the gross annual income, and *after* all payments are made on any mortgage loans. It's the *cash* that is left to *flow* into your pocket. Then there is *pre-tax cash flow* and *after-tax* (after depreciation) *cash flow*.

Let's look at the following example of an annual operating statement after one year of ownership:

For property at ___14022 S. School St., Riverdale, IL___

Year ended ___12-31-79___

Purchase price ___$170,000___

Down payment ___$ 15,000___

Gross rental income	$29,800	
Other income	1,440	
Total gross income		$31,240
Less: Property taxes	6,800	
Utilities	1,100	
Insurance	900	
Maintenance	660	
Independent contract	1,200	
Total operating expenses	$10,660	
Mortgage payments, 1st	14,400	
2nd	1,220	
Total mortgage payments	15,620	
Total cash outlay	26,280	26,280
Net cash flow before income tax		4,960

Income Tax Computation

Total income		31,240
Less: Total operating expenses	10,660	
Total mortgage interest	13,200	
Depreciation—building	7,000	
Furnace and appliances depreciation	4,000	
Total deductible expense		34,860
Net taxable income		(Loss—3,620)

Note that the cash flow of $4,960 is a 33 percent return on your investment of $15,000 (the down payment). But that isn't all. You not only keep that cash flow, but you still have a paper loss of $3,620.

You would subtract this $3,620 from your personal income before figuring your tax. (With income-producing property you get to write-off/deduct interest, operating expenses, and depreciation, all covered in depth in a later chapter.)

There is still more! The total mortgage payments were $15,620, and the interest portion was $13,200. That means the mortgage reduction was $2,420 (paid on the principal). So your equity has increased by $2,420.

And finally—at 10% appreciation per year, the property has increased in value by $17,000 in this one year.

Now let's figure the *real* return on investment as follows:

1. Cash flow (into pocket)	$ 4,960
2. Tax shelter (if you are in the 50% bracket you save ½ of $3,620 loss)	1,810
3. Mortgage reduction	2,420
4. Appreciation at 10%	17,000
Total gain	$26,190

On a $15,000 down payment, $26,190 means a 174% *total return on investment*. ($26,190 divided by $15,000 = 174%.) If you can realize that kind of return on an investment, you are truly beating inflation.

Don't let down payments get you down. In later chapters you will learn many ways to borrow what you need. In the meantime, let's look at another investment and its yield: An 18-unit, brick, middle-income apartment.

1. Price: $340,000. Down payment $34,000
   Net annual cash flow (after mortgage payment) $8,000
   Income tax liability (deduct if taxable income is
   positive; otherwise add to loss)   – 18,000 loss
   Net income *after* tax (loss on paper only)   – 10,000
2. First year
   Tax bracket 33% (tax saved on $10,000)   3,333
   Total spendable cash 1st year   11,333
3. Annual return on cash invested:
   A. Before income tax

   $$\frac{\$8,000}{\text{Net annual pre-tax cash flow}} \div \frac{\$34,000}{\text{Cash down payment}} \times 100\% \quad 23\%$$

   B. After income tax:

   $$\frac{\$11,333}{\text{Net spendable cash after-tax}} \div \frac{\$34,000}{\text{Cash down payment}} \times 100\% \quad 33\%$$

   C. After tax and adding mortgage reduction to
      cash flow:

Cash flow	$8,000
Mortgage reduction 1st year	3,600
Income tax credit	3,330
Total return	14,930

   $$\frac{\$14,930}{\text{Total return}} \div \frac{34,000}{\text{Cash down payment}} \times 100\% \quad 43\%$$

What can be nicer than to make a profit and keep it!

Don't forget the profit from appreciation. Assuming 10% appreciation per year (which could be higher or lower, of course, in coming years), the property increased in value $34,000. If sold with that increase, a $34,000 appreciation based on $34,000 cash investment equals 100% return. If you add that 100% appreciation to the above figure of 43% return, you make a 143% total return on your original cash investment. (Even a 5% appreciation gives you a 93% return!)

So far we have looked at buildings owned only one year. We have not yet considered the impact of annual rent increases. If you raised the rent on one apartment $25 a month, that equals $300 for the year. The value of a building usually increases 10 times that annual rent increase; that means the value of the building has increased $3,000.

The following chart projects rent increases over a period of 15 years, on a building purchased in 1976. Bear in mind that expenses do not increase in the same proportion as rents. We are not figuring for rent controlled areas.

FIGURING THE BUYS

Description	Purchased 1976	Today 1983	Projected 1985	Projected 1990
Apartment #1—1 Bedroom	$ 160	$ 235	$ 445	$ 695
Apartment #2—Efficiency	$ 140	$ 200	$ 400	$ 580
Apartment #3—1 Bedroom	$ 160	$ 235	$ 445	$ 695
Apartment #4—3 Bedrooms	$ 230	$ 350	$ 560	$ 860
Apartment #5—2 Bedrooms	$ 190	$ 275	$ 495	$ 780
Apartment #6—2 Bedrooms	$ 190	$ 275	$ 495	$ 780
Apartment #7—1 Bedroom	$ 160	$ 235	$ 445	$ 695
Apartment #8—1 Bedroom	$ 160	$ 235	$ 445	$ 695
Apartment #9—1 Bedroom	$ 160	$ 235	$ 445	$ 695
Apartment #10—2 Bedrooms	$ 190	$ 275	$ 495	$ 780
Apartment #11—2 Bedrooms	$ 190	$ 275	$ 495	$ 780
Apartment #12—2 Bedrooms	$ 190	$ 275	$ 495	$ 780
Total Monthly	$ 2,120	$ 3,100	$ 5,660	$ 8,815
Annual gross	$25,440	$37,200	$67,920	$105,780

If you are now renting your shelter, instead of owning it, you better believe this is the kind of rental future you have ahead of you.

Note that the rents on the chart almost tripled in the first ten years because of the high rate of inflation in the last part of the 70's and first half of the 80's. The value of a $200,000 apartment building would probably have tripled to $600,000 in the same period of time.

You say you can't believe it? Remember that beautiful 3 bedroom brick home that sold for $18,000 in 1968? It cost $75,000 in 1983. That same leap in value happens to large pieces of property. The dollar amount is just that much greater.

In our experience, it has been easier to find a building that will pay for itself among the larger pieces of property—4-flats, 6-flats and 12-flats. By pay-for-itself, we mean that the income will pay for all expenses and payments.

It has also been our experience that you will probably get a better buy when you find a building, in a good area, that needs some cosmetics—that is painting, landscaping, and minor fix-ups. (We will discuss improving your investments in greater detail in a later chapter.) We have found that the "ugly duckling"—the building that has been allowed to run down—will usually be sold for less and has the greatest potential for increasing in value in the shortest period of time. You want buildings that have been mismanaged, and whose owners must sell. If you find a building that has major problems, you will have to then decide whether your investment is still financially feasible. The answer may depend on whether you have the financial resources and/or skills to make your building profitable.

INSPECTING PROPERTIES

After reviewing the financial statement, and deciding that a particular property is a good possible investment, your next step will be to inspect that property. You don't have to be a professional appraiser or contractor to determine whether a property is in good or fair shape. Besides, your personal inspection is probably superior to the seller's evaluation of the condition of the building. During your inspection you should make written notes of the following features:

Exterior

1. Note the first impression—the appeal of the building upon your arrival. Try to view it as a prospective tenant might.

2. Note anything that looks unusual to you—that catches your eye for whatever reason.

3. Look for tuckpointing, structural problems, lot layout, trees, pitch of landscape, parking, amenities (such as tennis courts, pools, garages, balconies).

4. Note the upkeep of the lot.

5. Check the window views (what do they look out on); their storms and screens, broken glass.

6. Check surrounding properties; adjacent lots.

Interior

1. Does outside door provide security? Shut tight to keep air and water out?

2. Condition of hallways: carpeting; grafitti on walls or doors; any holes in plaster or drywall; heated or not; peeling paint might mean a moisture problem. Do hall windows have curtains or stained-glass to keep sun out?

3. Check the ceiling at the top floor of the building for any water-leak marks.

Inside Apartments

1. Try to view as many units as possible.

2. Look at the type of heat, type of energy used.

3. Note general condition of unit—does it need paint?

4. Is there air conditioning? Window unit?

5. How many electrical outlets per room. Are they overloaded?

6. Check for drafts, window caulking, and condition of wood around the window frame and sill.

7. Flush all toilets—look for water leaks, dripping water, energy-saving shower heads, pressure at faucets; How long does it take the hot water to get hot?

8. Appliances: Are they owner-owned? If so, check color and condition.

9. Note number of rooms, bedrooms, baths.

10. Ask owner about water heater, heating and cooling systems, roof. Are there warranties and/or guarantees on any appliances or improvements.

11. Ask the tenants about the roof, porches, heating system.

12. Try to find out how the tenants feel about their building, their likes and dislikes. Many times they will give you a history of the building, as well as information about other tenants and the owners.

If you are not certain about the condition of any of the above, it's best to have your attorney add a protection clause in your contract (see contract chapter) which calls for an inspection by professionals.

The following Property and Unit Analysis Sheets should speed up your collection of information and ensure that you don't overlook any facts.

PROPERTY ANALYSIS

Address: _____

Age: _____

Condition: _____

Construction: _____Lot size: _____ × _____

# of units: _____ Building size_____ × _____

Flood control (type) _____ Sewerage:____Overhead ____Septic

Parking: ____On street ____Off street ____Garages

____Carports ____# of spaces ____Sq. footage parking area

Heating: ____Gas ____Electric ____Boiler (Age, condition) _____

____Forced air ____Baseboard ____Hot water

____Radiant   Energy saving devices _____

Cooling: ____Gas C/A ____Elec. C/A ____Window ____Built-in

Electric: ____Individual units ____Individual meters ____Common

Who pays? ____Landlord ____Tenant

Circuit breakers (location) _____   Fuses (location) _____

Plumbing: ____Sump pump ____Hot water heater (age, condition)

Roof: ____type ____age _____condition

Porches: ____enclosed ____exposed

Walk-up_____ Elevator_____

Carpeting: ____Vestibules ____Units ____Per room

_____Color _____Condition

Storm windows & screens: _____

Basements: ____Common ____Units

Laundry room:____# machines ____Individual units ____Common

____Gas ____Electric ____Mfr. or repair company

Recreation amenities: ____Pool ____Balconies ____Club house

____Tennis ____Sunning area ____Other

Unit Analysis

Appliances: # per unit_____ Age_____

Type	Energy Used	Condition	Color
Stove	_____	_____	_____
Refrigerator	_____	_____	_____
Dishwasher	_____	_____	_____
Disposal	_____	_____	_____

Kitchens: _____Eat in _____Cabineted

Dining rooms: # (total)   Size_____ ×_____

Closets: # per unit

Balconies: Total #

Unit type	No.	Baths	# of Rooms	Sq. ft.	View	Rent
1 Bedroom	_____	_____	_____	_____	_____	_____
2 Bedroom	_____	_____	_____	_____	_____	_____
3 Bedroom	_____	_____	_____	_____	_____	_____
Efficiency/ Studio	_____	_____	_____	_____	_____	_____

Notes:

WHAT YOU SHOULD KNOW ABOUT SELLERS

When you have negotiated with enough sellers you will discover that they are more worried about the purchase price and the down payment than they are about the percent of interest or the number of years that the contract runs. *Use this fact to your advantage because you should be most interested in a low interest rate and a long term mortgage.*

Don't take the seller's word on the condition of the building. Talk to the tenants and find out more about the building than the owner even knows. Sellers love to tell you what they have done to improve the building since they purchased it—not what is needed.

Take your time and check things out. Get proof when it comes to taxes, expenses and income. When a seller seems too anxious to sell, better ask yourself what's wrong with this "buy." Don't just look at the plusses and close your eyes to the negatives.

Remember a good lawyer and a good sales contract are vital when purchasing "a good buy."

6
FINANCING
Doing It Conventionally

6
FINANCING
Doing It Conventionally

There are numerous sources of funds for investing in real estate, but they fall into two main groups: conventional sources and not-so-conventional—the latter now termed "creative." Conventional sources provide little or no seller involvement. Creative sources provide mostly seller involvement, in various combinations.

This chapter will cover the conventional avenues of funding available to you, while chapter seven will describe various ways the seller can participate. The variety of financing possibilities means you needn't limit yourself to any particular type of property under the misguided notion that you'll have trouble financing other types. Because each seller has different needs and desires, it's entirely possible that you can come up with financing tailored to fit any seller of any property. When seeking a loan from a conventional source, you will increase your chances for success by putting together a package. A package is the sum total of information about yourself and your investment. It's everything your banker-loan source—wants to know and may not bother to ask. (Details follow.)

The following sources of money, and types of mortgages and loans, should give you an idea of the variety of conventional financing available. (Later in the chapter we describe in greater detail the more common types.)

SOURCES OF MONEY
- Banks; Savings & Loans
- Government loans (F.H.A., V.A.)
- Insurance companies
- Mortgage companies
- Joint ventures:
  Real Estate Investment Trusts (REIT)

    Syndications

    Partnerships

- Credit unions
- Private financial institutions (such as F.N.M.A.)
- Wealthy individual investors

TYPES OF LOANS

- Fixed rate mortgage
- Renegotiable rate mortgage (RRM)
- Variable rate mortgage (VRM)
- Graduated payment mortgage (GPM)
- Buy-downs
- Pledged accounts
- Equity loans
- Blanket mortgage
- Second mortgages (check local laws for any restrictions)
- Interim loans (such as credit cards)

A "PACKAGE" IS YOUR PASSPORT TO MONEY

A package is your entry into the competition for money from a bank or savings and loan, or some other source. By putting together a package, you show the financial world that you are a professional and that you are in control of your investments to make money.

Remember, the bank's loan officers often don't know you or anything about your investment. While an appraisal of the property provides them with some basis for a decision, bankers tend to loan money as much on the basis of trust *in* people as *on* the dollar value of property. They essentially are making a paper decision based on the credit you have built up with them over the years, or through the methods we discussed earlier.

Most people who apply for funds simply walk in with a contract they have negotiated on some property, fill out the application forms, and then return home to await a yes or no on their loan. A package gives you an edge. It not only increases your chances for success, but enhances your professional image, whether the loan is granted or not.

You should create a package even if you expect the property to be owner-financed. Sooner or later you'll need the banks (especially when interest rates drop). You may need additional funds to refinance or obtain a second mortgage, or for improvements.

Your package should include the following:

Personal Data:

- An updated copy of your credit report.
- A financial statement that shows your assets and liabilities. (Everything you own; everything you owe.)
- Verification of your employment, including:
  Your gross income; years on the job; description of your job duties. (Do not hedge about your work—people will accept the value of what you do if you yourself value it.)
- Personal references from employers, creditors, other bankers, friends, church, etc.
- How other investments have fared through your efforts. (You can be honest because it's understood we're all human and make mistakes.)
- Your future goals both personally and through your investments.

Investment Data

- The sales contract—signed by all parties involved.
- Property information:

  Legal description; size of building and units; lot size; parking; type of heating and cooling; construction; amenities; improvements; financial sheet with rent and security deposit breakdown; copies of the leases showing stability of the building's income.
- Expenses (copies of the past three-years' records, if possible).

- Your plans to raise income and lower expenses, thereby increasing the total value of the building.
- Comparables on similar types of properties that have sold recently to show loan officer that you have found a good buy.

Type all the information neatly, include pictures, and enclose the pages in a binder. Make several copies so that you can apply at several different lending institutions.

Whether you need the loan, or already have concluded a purchase on contract, it's to your advantage for the banks to have this information on record so that in three to five years you can return and show them just how well you did in terms of raising the value of the property and increasing the net income. In fact, when you drop your copies off, you can tell them you'll be back to see them for money in a few years. They'll be glad to see you. Note: Be careful not to go to the lender of a contract sale property for a possible due-on-sale clause in the seller's mortgage.

WHAT YOU SHOULD KNOW ABOUT BANKERS (ACCORDING TO BILL JOSEPH)

When I started out I got so frustrated and hurt when bankers denied me a loan because I had no collateral. I'd ask how they expected me to have collateral when they wouldn't give me a mortgage to buy real estate. They'd say, "I'm sorry, but that's bank policy," or give me the following favorite excuses:

- "We're not loaning money at this time."

  (You can sit in the bank for an hour and someone will walk out with the loan you wanted.)

- "Are you going to live in the property? No? Sorry, that's one of our bank's requirements when we give a loan."

  (You can find a landlord with 12 pieces of property and know he can't be living in all of them at the same time.)

- "We want a 25 percent (or 30 percent or 40 percent) down payment."

  (That's more than other banks and more than they ask of someone else.)

How do you get around these run-arounds?

1. Have accounts at a number of different banks. One of a banker's favorite questions is, "Do you have an account with our bank? We loan money only to people who deal with us."

2. Savings and Loans give out more mortgages than banks do and with lower down payments in general—so concentrate on them.

3. Try to find out which loan officer has real estate of his/her own and is a landlord. He or she will help you more and understand what you mean when you say the cash flow is $15,000 per year on a building.

4. Always deal with the same banker in a particular bank.

5. Remember that when a banker is discussing your credit application, he is really qualifying you and concerned about your ability to pay back the loan. If he makes too many bad loans he won't remain at that bank too long. So present your package to him, understanding that you are competing for money in today's market. Have your facts and figures handy with a well-planned portfolio on the property. Look and act in control of your business.

6. Shop around for the best terms.

The Loan Process

When you apply to a bank or savings and loan, with your package, you will probably encounter the following procedure:

1. You present your package and a copy of a dated contract signed by all parties—seller(s), buyer(s), trustees, etc.

2. You fill out a loan application and a financial statement; a fee is required.

3. The bank then runs a credit check on you and gets an appraisal on the property; a fee is charged for these activities.

4. When the bank receives the above reports, a committee meets to approve or disapprove loans. Your package also will be considered at this time.

5. If approved, a letter of acceptance is sent you.

6. You must then fill out and sign mortgage papers.

7. A title search is ordered by the lender. Sometimes a survey is also ordered, depending on the lender. Some will accept a year-old survey, others always insist on a new one.

8. Upon receipt of the results of the title search and survey, the bank informs all parties that they are ready to close so that a closing date can be agreed upon.

9. Closing takes place, either with attorneys and concerned parties or in escrow as explained in the chapter on selling techniques.

TYPES OF MORTGAGES AND LOANS

Due-On-Sale Mortgages

Many mortgages have a written provision that requires the mortgager (owner) to pay off the balance owed a mortgage if the owner sells the mortgaged property. (Sometimes the provision requires the owner to get the approval of the lender if the property is sold.) Therefore, most owners believed that if they sold their property on installment contracts—Articles of Agreement for Warranty Deed, etc.—and if they retained the deed until an agreed-upon-time in the future, they had not yet "sold" the property. After all they hadn't received full payment, and they still retained the deed as proof of ownership. Therefore, they need not notify the lender or pay off the old mortgage.

Recent court decisions have decided otherwise. They have stated that a properly worded due-on-sale clause, as required by state or federal law, is enforceable because a sale has taken place whether the deed changes hands or not. Furthermore, the issue went all the way to the Supreme Court where it was ruled that a due-on-sale clause in mortgages with federally charted savings and loans are enforceable, regardless of what state regulations might say to the contrary.

Your attorney is the person to decide if a particular mortgage document—your own or someone else's—is so worded that the lender could call in the balance of the mortgage. (See the section on a lease purchase for a legal method to overcome the due-on-sale problem.)

Many lenders, of course, want to get rid of older, lower-rate mortgages. They also want to avoid court costs and publicity involved should they go after sellers who are keeping the old mortgage in violation of the due-on-sale clauses. Nevertheless, they are trying to search out such sellers and will often, though not always, offer them a new mortgage at a higher rate but one that is still below the current rate. Other lenders are notifying their mortgagees (owners of old mortgages) that they have instituted special financing arrangements and fees if they should sell (or have secretly sold) their properties. The usual arrangement is some form of blended mortgage. For instance, some lenders allow the owner to keep the old interest rate, or a lower-than-market rate, but increase the monthly payments so as to pay the loan off in a shorter period of time. (See financing chapter for blended mortgages.)

Fixed Rate Mortgage

Almost all mortgages used to be of the fixed-rate type. That is, they carried an interest rate that was fixed for the term of the mortgage, usually 25 to 30 years. Buyers liked them because they not only knew that their monthly payments wouldn't change, but that in all likelihood they would eventually be paying back the balance owed in cheaper dollars because of inflation. Bankers didn't mind because they paid a lesser rate for savings out of which they made loans at higher rates. But banks and savings and loans no longer like to offer these mortgages because of the recent roller-coaster interest rate changes that forced them to pay out higher rates on savings than they were receiving on old, low rate mortgages. Now, lenders that will offer a fixed rate mortgage usually will charge a much higher interest rate. For instance, they may charge 16 to 17 percent for a fixed rate mortgage, but only 13 percent for a variable rate mortgage although fixed rate mortgage interest rates have been falling (explained later).

Graduated Equity Mortgage (GEM)

The Graduated Equity Mortgage is also referred to as a Rapid Payment Mortgage (RPM), and is a variation of the Fixed Rate Mortgage. With this type of financing the interest rate doesn't change, but the monthly payments do increase a certain percent per year, usually from 3 to 5 percent. All of the increased payment, however, is applied to the principal, thus reducing its balance. In this way the loan is paid off at a quicker rate. With this method a 30-year mortgage could be paid off in 16.5 to 18.5 years. Your equity is growing rapidly with the higher payments, hence the title of Graduated Equity Mortgage or Rapid Payment Mortgage. While the rapid growth of equity is a plus, this type of mortgage is more suitable to a buyer who expects his income to grow as fast or faster than his monthly payments.

Adjustable Rate Mortgage (ARM)

An Adjustable Rate Mortgage is one given by banks and savings and loans which allow the interest rate to increase or decrease based on an index such as the Federal Home Loan Bank Boards Index. This index involves the national average of monthly mortgage interest rates. The lender must notify the borrower in writing 90 days prior to any change and must include notice of the new payment amounts. These interest rates are fixed for the first three years, then adjusted each year according to the index. Points will be charged. Some lenders may offer slightly lower rates in the beginning to attract borrowers, so shop around for the best rates and terms.

Variable Rate Mortgage (VRM)

The Variable Rate Mortgage (another form of the ARM) allows for changes in the interest rate depending on selected indices, such as the one mentioned above, or the yield on U.S. Treasury Bills, or the average cost of money for savings and loans. The rates could change every six months, and some loans limit the increase or decrease to a maximum of one half percent a year or two and one half percent over the term of the loan. You probably will need an accountant to figure out which index is the best for your situation. You also want to limit the number of increases and their amount, if possible. Points are again levied on the mortgage amount being borrowed.

Graduated Payment Mortgage (GPM)

A graduated payment mortgage is of most use to those who find it presently difficult to afford high monthly payments, but expect their income to be greater in the future. With the GPM, the mortgage payments rise gradually over a period of years, then level off and remain steady for the balance of the term of the mortgage. The difference between what the monthly payment should be, and the lower amount you're actually paying, is added back on to the loan balance. The FHA has a graduated payment program number 245 which allows for the same procedure, but with little money down, and all other terms under FHA mortgages applying.

Buy-Downs

This type of mortgage has been used by many contractors with new construction. The "buy-down" has filtered down, however, to sellers of all types of real estate: homes, condominiums, and multi-family. The seller arranges to obtain a mortgage through a lender, such as bank or savings and loan, at an interest rate anywhere from 2 to 4 percent below current rates, for a short period of time. The seller is actually paying the difference between the current rate and the lower one in order to make it easier for the buyer to qualify for the purchase and to make payments in the earlier years. The number of years depends on the terms of the contract—anywhere from one to seven as a rule. That interest rate is temporary, however, and the buyer must renegotiate a new rate with the lender at the end of the buy-down period or it might automatically increase at a given time.

The seller pays this difference in rates out of the proceeds of the sale. Therefore you must make sure that the property has not been over-valued, and over-priced, to compensate the seller for his buy-down. As with all mortgages, points will be charged and approval given by the bank for all terms.

Federal Housing Administration (FHA) Loans

FHA loans, which are insured by the Federal Housing Administration, are commonly thought to be available only to poor people. The truth is that anyone can obtain an FHA mortgage for property up to four units, owner occupied. The loans require little money down, at below market interest rates, usually have fixed terms, and are assumable at the existing rate. A mortgage insurance payment must be paid by the buyer on his payments if less than 20 percent is placed as a down payment. The seller and buyer may now split the points charged by the lender. They will now consider loans to non-owner occupied investors. The maximum mortgage amounts available on any property will vary from state to state and from year to year. Check with your realtor and loan officer for any recent changes in FHA requirements.

Veterans Administration (VA) Loans

A VA mortgage is guaranteed by the Veterans Administration. A veteran, with a certificate of eligibility, may purchase up to a four-unit, owner occupied building with no money down at below market interest rates. Each state has different maximum amounts that the veteran can borrow. Points are paid by the seller and vary as to the amounts. At the end of 1981, in the Chicago area, they were about one percent of the mortgage amount, the lowest we've seen, and it wasn't long before they increased. All VA mortgages are issued as long term fixed mortgages with due-on-sale clauses. The loans are then assumable at the existing rate by anyone, veteran or non-veteran. Usually the VA will not return the original buyer's Certificate of Eligibility until the original loan is paid off, thus may vets won't allow their mortgages to be assumed by a non-vet.

Private Loan (Interim) Sources

Private loan companies throughout the country, such as Household Finance Corp. (H.F.C.) advertise their willingness to lend money based on the equity in your home.

Mortgage Brokers usually act as a go-between to help you get your loan processed through a mortgage company or bank. Since they split the points paid to the mortgage company, you pay for their services by paying a premium for the loan.

Private individuals also advertise their readiness to loan money on property or buy up mortgages. Use caution when working with such individuals and do not sign anything until your attorney has seen and approved the papers. Don't be over-anxious—you could lose your money or property just by acting in a hurry.

Interest rates charged by private loan sources are high because they're not competitive. They, therefore, should be considered as sources of interim financing—a bridge loan.

Such loans are often used by condominium converters (as explained in greater detail in our chapter on condominiums). The loans are available at 2 percent above the prime interest rates for six months or a year. These loans have an option for renewal and often require only the payment of interest every six months or year. They are renewed only until the converter can obtain a regular mortgage. Their high interest rate is usually offset by the profit anticipated in condominium conversions.

Refinancing—the "Blended" Way

The first alternative that occurs to many property owners who wish to refinance the equity in their property is the second mortgage. It may or may not be a wise choice depending on the numbers (as we explain later). In any event, many mortgage documents don't allow the title holder to place a second mortgage on his properties. The lender may instead offer the possibility of refinancing through a "Blended Mortgage" (or "Weighted Mortgage"). This method may make sense for you if you currently have an old mortgage with a low interest rate. Your original lender can offer one or more of the following options:

1. Simply lump together the remaining balance of the old mortgage and the new money requested into one new loan at a higher rate than the old, but still below current market rates. If your old rate was 7 percent, they may offer you a new loan at 11 or 12 percent, if the current rates are 14 percent. They have "blended" the rates, depending on how much new money you're borrowing.

2. Bring the rate on the old mortgage up 2 to 4 percent above its existing rate; then loan the new money at the current rate of interest. The two amounts, old and new, are blended together to form a new in-between rate—higher than the old, lower than the new.

Some lenders have a minimum rate, such as 12 percent for the old mortgage balance, which could bring up the old rate more than 4 percent.

For example: A lender may say they will loan you up to 80 percent of the current value of your home, or $75,000 maximum, whichever is less. Your home is now worth $100,000 and your original mortgage was $30,000, but the maximum the bank will loan you is $75,000 at 12 percent interest with a 25-year amortization. Your payment will be $790.50 per month. Your current mortgage, at 7 percent with 25-year amortizaton, costs you $212.04 per month. Therefore, by refinancing you'll pay $578.46 a month more. Should you?

Let's find out. You have a chance to buy that 12-unit building for $300,000 at 9 percent interest with a net cash flow of $7,000 a year, or about $583.33 a month profit. That would take care of your new mortgage expense of $578.46 and leave you $4.87. Would you consider that a reasonable way to enter real estate investing? Actually, you could say you're making even more than that because your cash flow is taking care of your original mortgage payment of $212.04. So in essence you bought the $300,000 building with no money down, even though you put down $45,000 borrowed on the equity in your house. In other words, it was all borrowed money—or 100% Financing.

On the other hand, your lender may be willing to bring up your old rate on your mortgage balance to 11 percent and charge you 16 percent on the new money. The $30,000 balance at 7 percent, and $212.04 a month, would increase to 11 percent and $294.30 a month. The $45,000 new money (to equal $75,000) would be loaned at 16 percent interest, 25-year amortization, or $611.55 a month. Your grand total would be $905.85 per month.

When you blend $30,000 at 11 percent with $45,000 at 16%, you come up with an overall rate of about 14% interest, which is still below market rates.

Now let's compare that outlay with the same 12-unit property figures: We still have $583.33 a month cash flow. Subtract that from the $905.85 per month new mortgage cost, and that leaves $322.52 a month to be paid out-of-pocket. But not entirely. Remember you had been paying $212.04 on the original mortgage on your house. So if you bought the building, you would be laying out only an extra $110.48 a month, or about $1,325.72 a year. Chances are you're in a high tax bracket and can use the tax shelter advantages, cutting your cash outlay even more. Also consider that the property will probably appreciate in value more in one year than you may be paying out: and you'll be paying the loans back with cheaper dollars (even if inflation drops, it doesn't disappear).

The question then is: can you afford to pay the higher payments or—can you afford *not* to buy the property? When considering what you can afford, don't forget that you will be charged points on the borrowed money, about 3 percent, and the loan costs including credit check, appraisal fee, etc. You should at least try to get the lender to waive some fees in order to keep your business.

One last option exists that is very similar to a second mortgage. Your lender may allow you to keep your old mortgage at the old rate and add new money at the new rate. That means you'd still pay $212.04 on the $30,000 mortgage at 7 percent, plus $611.55 per month on the $45,000 borrowed at 16 percent. Your total payment would be $823.59 on a total loan of $75,000. That works out to a blended rate of around 12-5/8 percent. To return to the same 12-unit building, with its $583.33 a month profit, you would again have an out-of-pocket expense of $240.26 per month. But if you again deduct your original mortgage outlay of $212.04, then you really have an out-of-pocket expense of only $28.22 a month, or $338.64 a year—the price of owning that 12-unit building.

With a second mortgage at the same rate, the figures would be the same, the only difference being there would be two mortgages, instead of one.

Remember that the above figures don't include the tax shelter advantages of your investment. Nor is your equity sitting like a lump underneath your house. It's now earning you money. And all that $45,000 you borrowed isn't gone. You used $15,000 or so for expenses and protection, so you still have about $30,000 left over for another investment.

Your bank will probably cooperate in order to get your old 7 percent mortgage off its books. But be sure to check all figures and "blends" to see how they work in your specific case and within the guidelines of your mortgage.

You can also use the blended mortgage method with the institution that is holding the original mortgage on the property you wish to buy. In order to help the sale go through, they too might be willing to cooperate and get the old mortgage off their books. For example:

The seller has an old mortgage rate of 8 percent with a $50,000 mortgage balance. You purchase the property for $120,000 with $20,000 down, and need a $100,000 mortgage. You ask the lender to combine the seller's old mortgage of $50,000 with a new mortgage of $50,000. The lender will often raise the rate of the old mortgage to their minimum, let's say 12 percent, then loan you the second $50,000 at current rates of 16 percent. Then the two are blended together to give you an in between rate of about 13 to 14 percent on the $100,000 mortgage. As you can see, the less new money needed, the lower your overall payments on principal and interest will be. The bank will also charge you points on the new loan (an interest charge of 2 percent or more). Not a bad way for them to get rid of an older, lower-rate mortgage. They will still require, of course, that the buyer qualify for this loan. Don't forget that if rates should come down you will be able to refinance your property at a lower rate. Again payment of points will probably be required.

A.B.I.

Sometimes, if you find interest rates too high, it's possible to use up to 100 percent of your equity in your home or other property without having to refinance it or sell it. Instead, you give the seller an Assignment of Beneficial Interest (A.B.I.). An A.B.I. is essentially a promissory note that says you agree to pay the seller a certain amount of money toward the down payment. To protect himself, the seller then records a lien against your property as a second or third mortgage. This recorded lien prevents you from selling the property until you first pay off the note.

You repay the note to the seller as agreed upon in the original clause and/or later negotiations. Repayment can be in monthly payments, yearly balloon payments over a specified period of time, or one balloon payment at a date two or three years from closing. It's also possible to avoid paying interest on the A.B.I., or simple interest only; or you might make payments of interest only with a balloon payment after a specified period. All possibilities are negotiable, but you should include one of them in the original offer. In some cases it can be necessary, and effective, to add some cash to the A.B.I. that will cover the seller's closing cost.

Why would a seller accept an A.B.I.? Many sellers don't need a cash down payment, but they do need a buyer. They also need to know that you won't just walk away from your purchase because you have nothing of your own invested in it. With the A.B.I. the seller has the security of knowing that if you don't pay as agreed, you have something of value at stake—your home or other property. Something you don't want to lose. The A.B.I. and the recorded lien against your property give the seller the protection and security he needs.

Seller Refinancing

Sometimes a seller, in anticipation of a future sale, can refinance his property at below market rates. He would seek an assumable mortgage and borrow the most amount of money allowed. The buyer, then, would be able to assume that mortgage. If a seller has not already refinanced his property, you, the buyer, can suggest it, especially if your own credit is not yet good enough to obtain a large mortgage.

Another advantage of a seller refinancing occurred in the following situation:

An owner of a large rental apartment complex wanted to retire, but didn't want to sell his property, worth $2,000,000. He first made his son a co-owner, and then refinanced the building for over $1,000,000. He turned the responsibility for the payments over to his son. The father was able to retire on the $1,000,000 tax free because borrowed funds aren't taxable until the profit is realized through the sale of the property. The son received a building with a $1,000,000 equity, which he "paid for" by paying off the million dollar note out of the income proceeds. Both father and son split the tax write-offs.

Assuming an Existing Mortgage

When you assume an existing mortgage you have to pay the difference between what the seller owes and what price the seller wants for the property. For instance, to assume a $50,000 mortgage on a property now worth $70,000, you would have to come up with $20,000 cash. The seller could take back a second mortgage for part or all of that cash down payment. The benefit to the buyer in assuming a mortgage is in its usually lower interest rate and its availability.

Blanket Mortgage

A blanket mortgage involves more than one property. By using two or more properties for financing or refinancing, you can often maximize your loan amount, particularly when one of them has no mortgage, or a very small one. Not only does a blanket mortgage increase your lender's security, it also provides you with a much stronger position when negotiating the terms of your loan; often it allows you to obtain a lower interest rate than if you mortgaged each property separately. However, be careful when using a blanket mortgage because it ties up or encumbers two or more properties and makes it difficult to later split or separate the properties for individual sale.

A blanket mortgage lets you use 100% Financing because the equity of the additional property is used to secure the loan and allows you to borrow in excess of the value of the main property. For example: lenders usually allow up to 80 percent financing, thus requiring 20 percent to remain in the property as their security. For a $100,000 building, local lenders would loan a maximum of $80,000. Now let's say you have equity in vacant land or some other property difficult to refinance, whose appraised value is $60,000, with no mortgage. You provide the lender with the security of a blanket mortgage—combining the two properties, and they finance 70 to 80 percent of the total package, or of $160,000. The numbers would be as follows:

$160,000	$160,000
70%	80%
$112,000	$128,000

By using your vacant lot to add security to your purchase, you achieved 100% Financing for your new building.

You might well consider a blanket mortgage when you've found a good buy with a great future potential, but with a currently negative cash flow. A case like this might occur with property that has long term leases at concessionary (low) rates. Even if you got a super buy with great terms (good price, below market interest, etc.) you still wouldn't be able to create a positive cash flow. But you can see that within a short period of time you will be able to raise income and lower expenses thus raising the value of the property and creating a positive cash flow.

A blanket mortgage would provide the added funds necessary to cover the negative cash flow until the leases can be renewed at higher amounts and income raised in other ways. The added borrowed funds mean no cash has to come out of your pocket to cover the negative cash flow. You should, of course, have some reserve to protect yourself against a longer than anticipated negative cash flow.

We recommend that by and large you avoid such negative situations in order to limit failure and maintain control of your investments to maximize your results. But if you need additional tax write-offs, and if you can afford a short period of loss, you could consider special situations as described above. In any case, check with your accountant to establish the safest position.

Shared Equity—Shared Appreciation

Let's say that you find a really good buy but don't have all the financial resources to put the transaction together. Some lenders, such as banks, savings and loans, insurance companies, and even private individuals, may be willing to loan you money on a shared equity arrangement. You should present the property, with your package, in much the same way as the real estate agent probably presented it to you to attract your interest. Then, based on the cash flow and future potential, as described in the documents, the lender may see a way for them to get a piece of the action—besides the interest payments.

You will probably feel elated at their interest, taking it as proof that you have put something of value together. This feeling may be short-lived, once you learn of the terms. They could offer you a not-so-below-market interest rate of say 12 percent to 14 percent, and in return ask for as much as 50 percent of the profit (maybe more) based on the future value of the property. They, the lender, often refuse to be responsible for management improvements, capital improvements, such as a new boiler or roof, etc. They not only refuse to pay such costs, but probably won't credit you with those costs when the profit is split. And speaking of profit—they won't want to wait too long for that profit. They usually want their money within three, four, or five years, which can force you to sell before you want to. But—if you want the property badly enough, this is an alternative way to go.

A Pledged Account as Security

Loan Officers sometimes disagree with buyers and sellers about their ability to handle a certain size loan and monthly payments. In other words, a bank may limit the size of your mortgage because it says you can only afford to pay back $2,500 a month. You, on the other hand, know that given the circumstances of the property, you can afford to pay back $3,000 a month. You need that higher mortgage, and higher payments, in order to buy the property.

In such a case, the seller may be willing to cooperate to the extent of a pledged account. First check with your banker to see if he will loan you the funds you need if someone else opens an account and pledges it as security. Then find out what the seller intends to do with the down payment monies and/or profits from the sale. Often, in order to complete the sale, and because the seller agrees that you should be able to make the higher monthly payments, he will be willing to pledge an account of $5,000 or so, which will draw interest at the current rate.

In return, the bank allows you the larger mortgage, and larger monthly payment, because they hold the seller's pledged account as security. Should you not be able to make the payment, they can remove the necessary amount from that account. The most the seller can lose, if he misjudged your ability to pay, is the $5,000, and he may consider that a small loss in return for a cash sale, and the opportunity to get his equity out of the property.

After a certain time the pledged account, or loan, is considered paid and the seller gets it back. It's also possible to arrange for the money in the account to be released gradually as you make your mortgage payments.

Co-Mortgagees

With ever-increasing interest rates and credit difficulties, young people and singles often find it hard to qualify for mortgages. A co-mortgagee, usually parents or relatives, can help by allowing their income and assets to become the basis for the loan. The banker is then assured that in the case of default, they will be responsible for the payments.

Family members, too, can open a pledged account, as described, with the consent of the banking institution.

Creative Down Payment Financing

Whatever you have of value may mean the difference between your obtaining a desired piece of property or not. You may have equity in your home, or little saved but a good income and credit; or you may put together a down payment by refinancing or using your car, boat, summer cottage, recreational vehicle, stocks, gold, etc. Some of the following sources should be considered short-term because of premium rates charged. Some sources can be combined.

Short-term Loan Sources

Private loan companies throughout the country, such as Household Finance Corporation, give personal loans on cars, furniture, and other luxury items, but they usually require a lien on your property to secure such loans. You will probably pay market rates for funds you borrow, so don't overextend yourself.

You can also ask the seller to allow you to place items such as jewelry, etc., with an escrow agent as security in place of a down payment. Of course all items need to be appraised.

You may be able to borrow on your credit cards. Many banks issue Visa and MasterCards with a credit limit as high as $1,000 or more. The interest, though deductible, is extremely high and such loans should be used with caution and only for a short term. You don't want to lose the credit you worked so hard to achieve.

Insurance policies and credit unions are often good sources of short term loans at more reasonable interest rates.

If you've established a good line of credit, you may be able to borrow $5,000 each from three banks you deal with. Or you might have some assets such as Treasury Bills or bonds that can be held by the bank and borrowed against.

Loans Based on Equity

Suppose that after trying all the methods described earlier you still don't have enough cash for the down payment. One of the best sources for most investors is the equity that has built up in their own homes. Your equity is the difference between what you still owe on your mortgage and what your home is worth on today's market. (As we'll show later, you can also use the equity the seller has built up in the property you are buying.)

There are several ways to use equity as a source of funds:

- Refinancing or second mortgages (blended mortgages)
- Assignment of Beneficial Interest (ABI)
- Seller refinancing
- Private loan sources
- Exchanges or trades (in which buyer and seller exchange equities)
- Seller Refinancing
- Private loan sources
- Exchanges or trades (in which buyer and seller exchange equities)

Partnerships

A partnership can be an advantage in the following situations:

1. You don't have any money and can find a partner who will buy

real estate with you on a 50/50 agreement. He supplies the money for the down payment and you supply the managing skills to run and operate the building complex.

2. You'd rather just invest the money and leave the management to somebody experienced and capable.

3. Together you should have twice the borrowing power. Banks also feel safer when they get two or three names on a loan agreement.

If you decide on a partnership, your best tool is a clear and fair agreement drawn up by an attorney. All the details should be spelled out in advance.

We have found that partnerships tend to fall apart because the two owners fail to agree. For example, one wants to fix up the building and the other doesn't want to spend the money. One wants to sell because he needs the money and the other wants to hold on for a tax write-off. The well-drawn agreement can at least anticipate and ease some of these differences.

General and Limited Partnerships

The general partner or partners have the responsibility for real estate property and also the liability for future costs. A general partner has the least amount of his own money invested and generally makes the most in profits if he does his job well, and if the building eventually sells for a good profit.

Many people prefer to be limited investors or partners because they don't want the responsibility and are afraid to handle the problems of real estate ownership. If you are the investor, you'd best examine the background of the general partner to whom you are trusting your money.

As long as people need to borrow money, and other people are willing to lend it, some kind of financing will always be available. If you are persistent and professional about your loan seeking, you will find the right combination to fit the seller's and your needs. So find that good buy, put together your package, and negotiate as close to 100% Financing as you can, according to our guidelines. Then you will discover for yourself the incomparable advantages of investing in real estate.

7
CREATIVE FINANCING
Doing It With The Seller

7

CREATIVE FINANCING
Doing It With The Seller

Unless you are willing and able—and foolish enough—to pay a premium price and interest rate for real estate, most financing today includes some seller involvement. Therefore, the first and major part of this chapter concentrates on the various ways the seller can participate.

You may find some owners who have never heard about seller financing, or know very little about its variations. That means your primary duty, and method, will be to educate your sellers. You have to show them the benefits that accrue *to them* if they finance the sale as you have structured it.

CONTRACT SALE

We'd best first clear up the definitions of some terms that are often used interchangeably, but don't really mean the same thing to everyone concerned.

A "Contract Sale" can be called any one of the following:

- Land Contract
- Contract for Deed
- Installment Agreement for Warranty Deed
- Installment Agreement
- Articles of Agreement for Warranty Deed
- Purchase Money Mortgage

All of these involve owner financing to some extent. But—an important but—in all but one the seller holds the deed until the final payment of the balloon note. The exception is the "Purchase Money

Mortgage," in which the deed does pass to the buyer at closing.

DEED VS. TITLE

Many times people interchange the words "deed" and "title." Title conveys interest in the property, whereas deed conveys ownership of the property. Usually when a person says he wants title to the property, he really means he wants the deed—or ownership.

As you can see, the seller and buyer have different preferences and needs for protection. The seller prefers the contract sale in which the deed doesn't pass to the buyer until he has received the balance of the money owed him. It is then easier for him to foreclose, or take back his property if the buyer defaults on payments. The seller, however, can give over the deed and still protect his interest by use of a trust (if state law permits), or by a lien on the property, as is done with a purchase-money mortgage.

You, as buyer, want the deed so that you can refinance or pyramid your equity. Without the deed, you only have a contractual interest in the property. You should record this position at the county recorder's office in your area to notify the world of your interest in the property. The seller cannot then sell the property again to another party because when the title is searched it will show your lien (interest in) the property. In order to be certain of protecting yourself in the terms of the contract, we recommend the use of an attorney and accountant in all real estate transactions.

In all sales, but particularly contract sales, your attorney should check the seller's mortgage documents for a due-on-sale clause so that you won't have to worry about the seller's mortgagee calling in the unpaid balance *after* you already have bought the property.

SELLER FINANCING

The proportions of seller financing may vary from a small second mortgage to 100% Financing (no money down), but the goal is always the same. The goal is maximum leverage to maximize your assets and results. Leverage, remember, means you must borrow: the *most* amount of money at the *lowest* possible interest rate for the *longest* period of time. The ultimate leverage is 100% Financing.

You want to borrow the most amount of money safely—meaning that you can repay—and that means "playing with the numbers." You must determine:

1. Your break-even point (or cash flow) on the property.

2. What the seller actually needs in the way of cash (a seller doesn't always need cash).

3. The highest interest rate that you can afford to pay with the least amount of money for your down payment.

(See the chapter on negotiating for detailed examples of "playing with the numbers.")

You should already have the information you need for step number one, such as the income and expenses for income-producing property. Let's assume you have decided to buy because the asking price is in the general area of ten times the net (income), or the seller might consider such a price. You also know your break-even point (how much cash is left over for mortgage payments after you subtract net expenses from net income). You are now ready to ask for the seller's financial involvement—if you know the seller's financial situation. If you don't, you must find out:

• Who holds their mortgage, if any?

• The interest rate of the mortgage.

• The balance of the mortgage.

• Is the mortgage assumable?

• Can the mortgage be rewritten at a slightly higher rate?

You must also know how willing or anxious the seller is to sell and what he intends to do with the profit he'd realize in a cash or conventional sale. Does he intend to:

• Re-invest?

• Retire?

• Buy another kind of business?

• Pay off debts?

- Buy an annuity?
- Put it in trust for a family member?
- Or have they already purchased a second home while their first is still on the market (a golden opportunity for you, the buyer, to step in, as explained later).

Sometimes you'll find out the seller's motives only by presenting a written offer or contract. (Naturally you'll protect yourself by including clauses as described in our contracts section.) Sellers tend to get enthused and open up once they're sure of your sincere interest as indicated by such a contract.

We cannot state it too strongly or too often: a seller's *motives* for selling mean *money* in the buyer's pocket. Your offer, therefore, depends on the seller's immediate needs as well as his long-term goals. Once you find out what the seller needs, try to satisfy those needs.

For instance: a seller may have to sell his real estate in order to pay off credit-card bills, or else lose his credit-rating. If you have a good credit rating, you might be able to assume the seller's debt in return for his equity interest in the property. Or you may be able to borrow the needed funds from your bank on a signature loan, without any collateral (an unsecured loan) and save a seller from foreclosure.

Sometimes a seller is seeking to cash-out of a property without recognizing all the ramifications. We usually tell such a seller that he must be awfully rich, or else he doesn't mind paying huge capital gains from the sale. (This applies to income property only, and does not affect residential property where it is possible to differentiate capital gains tax, as explained in the taxes and depreciation chapter.) Then we educate the seller. Often he doesn't realize that if he finances the property (through a contract sale or purchase-money mortgage) that he can spread the capital gains tax over a longer period of time. By so doing he usually can reduce his immediate tax liability (as explained in detail in the chapter on taxes and depreciation).

As the law now stands, when a seller sells property on contract (in effect becoming the bank or "paper man"), he pays capital gains taxes only on the down payment and that portion of the buyer's payments that are applied toward the reduction of the principal profit. His profit, therefore, is spread out over the years set by the sale terms. In other words, he doesn't pay the tax on his profit all at once, and a tax payment deferred is the same as a tax-free loan. If he received all the profit at one time (if he cashed-out as in a conventional sale), he could be pushed into a higher tax bracket—and pay higher taxes.

You could also point out why the seller might welcome a secure and regular monthly payment without the burden of caring for the property.

For instance: a couple who plan to retire, and whose income bracket will drop after retirement, might need added monthly income to supplement their social security, pension, or other income. By financing the sale, they gain extra monthly income on which they may pay less tax (lower tax bracket) than if they received all their profit at one time (a cash sale). If they plan to reinvest the profits in a non-real estate venture, the revenue from their new investment may not be as secure and regular as their monthly payments backed by the security of the property. After all, they know from experience the advantages of real estate over other types of investment.

INTERESTING INTEREST RATES

If the owner becomes the banker (by financing the mortgage himself), he not only makes money from the interest payments, but often makes a profit on the amount remaining in his original mortgage. If he continues to make payments on his old mortgage during the period of the contract sale, and if the original interest rate he's paying is less than what he is receiving from the contract-buyer, then he pockets the difference in interest. Such an arrangement is called a wrap-around mortgage which is possible if there are no restrictions on the first mortgage, such as a due-on-sale clause.

For example: if he still owes $50,000 at 7 percent, and you, the buyer, pay him 9 percent, then he makes 2 percent on the $50,000 balance, or $858.00 the first year. Of course, as his balance reduces on the old mortgage, that dollar amount does too.

Even if the seller finances the property at the *same* interest rate as he's currently paying, he still realizes a handsome profit. For example:

Seller's original mortgage is for $75,000 at 9 percent interest, 25 year amortization, with monthly payments of $630.00.

He gives you, the buyer, a $150,000 mortgage, also at nine percent. Your monthly payment is $1,260.00.

The seller would continue to pay his mortgage, and still would clear $630.00 per month. And he has no expenses because you, the buyer, would be responsible for all expenses on the property, including maintenance and management.

Of that $1,260.00 that you pay the seller, he pays capital gains taxes on the amount applied toward the profit portion of the principal. The portion that is interest is taxable as personal income. In other words, the $150,000 mortgage that the seller is carrying back from you is not all profit. Capital gains are owed only on the profit portion. To make absolutely sure that he pays only what he owes in taxes, the seller should always check with his accountant or lawyer.

If the seller asks for a higher interest rate, you should point out that the difference in after-tax dollars that he would receive is minimal. If that higher interest rate pushed the seller into an even higher tax bracket, he would pay even more in taxes and could end up receiving less in actual dollars. Note that on a $100,000 mortgage, an increase of 1 percent (from 9 percent to 10 percent) means $864.00 more the first year, *before* taxes. If the seller is in the 40 percent bracket, he nets only $518.40 in cash, or $43.20 a month. That extra $518.40 could also push him into the 50 percent bracket, netting him only $432.00, or $36 a month. Any other additional income he receives will also be taxed at the higher marginal rate.

There is a useful saying: Never argue price—just terms.

As you can see, in order to obtain the best leverage you have to negotiate favorable terms (see chapter on negotiations). You may have to give a seller his price in order to get a lower interest rate. In fact, sometimes you can make more money by offering *more* than the asking price, and receiving a much lower interest rate.

For example, the owner of a 6-unit building is asking $150,000 which you consider a very good price. But he wants 13 percent interest. It might be to your advantage to say, I'll give you $160,000 at ten percent interest. See what happens when you pay $10,000 *more* at the lower rate:

$150,000 at 13% interest $160,000 at 10% interest
$1,692.00 per month $1,454.40 per month
$20,304.00 per year $17,452.80 per year

You save $2,851.20 per year *and* have lower monthly payments.

In ten years you would save $28,512.00 just by using the lower interest rate. So it pays you, the buyer, to *pay more* in price and *save more* in interest—and dollars. You are also able to depreciate most of the $10,000 extra that you paid for the property. So it's good for the buyer; but why should the seller agree? He receives $10,000 more in profit which is taxed at the lower capital gains rate (maximum is only 20 percent, and his could be less). But on the $2,800 a year extra interest he would owe ordinary income tax, which could go as high as 50 percent depending on his tax bracket.

IMPUTED INTEREST

A seller can charge any interest he wishes, but the Internal Revenue Service (IRS) will impute an interest rate less than 9 percent if the seller charges a rate less than 9 percent, or states no rate, on installment contracts. In other words, they assume, for tax purposes, that the seller is actually receiving 10 percent interest.

On installment sales to family members, the IRS ruling states that the minimum allowable interest rate is 7 percent interest. Again, if no rate is stated in the contract, or if the rate is below 7 percent, the IRS will impute 9 percent to the seller.

These rulings don't mean that sellers cannot charge interest rates below 7 or 9 percent. It does mean that the sellers' interest income on installment sales will be computed as if they are receiving 9 or 10 percent interest.

You have probably seen advertisements by real estate agents or developers in which they offer property at below-market interest rates as low as 5 or 0 percent. Many of these offerings had short amortization periods (five to ten years) making the monthly payments higher, although the total cost of interest is less. Those sellers had to pay taxes, however, as if they received 10 percent interest. Many, therefore, raised their prices to compensate for the extra taxes paid.

The rule changes occurred as a means to raise tax revenue. All payments to the seller from the buyer are taxed two ways: profit is taxed as capital gains (60 percent exempt, 40 percent taxable, based on the tax bracket). Interest payments are taxed as ordinary income. Therefore, at 10 percent imputed interest the IRS receives more money than if the seller accepts less interest or the same amount of dollars as profit (selling price) and is taxed capital gains. (Zero percent interest is further discussed in the tax and depreciation chapter.)

BALLOONS

While you naturally want the longest period of time to repay a loan, you must realize that many sellers who agree to sell on an installment contract still don't want to finance the purchase over 20 or 30 years. They're willing to be the "paper man" for a while, but they want the balance owed them paid in full within a shorter amount of time. To achieve this the seller asks that the remaining balance be paid in full by a certain date. This arrangement is called a "balloon" or a "balloon note."

The balloon note doesn't increase your monthly payments. Those are structured or amortized over the longer period of time (25 to 30 years) to keep them low (affordable). For example:

You buy the property under the terms of an Article of Agreement for Warranty Deed, at 9 percent interest, amortized over 25 years. (The payments are figured as if the note will be paid back over 25 years.) But at the end of a certain period (three to five, or five to seven or more years—it's negotiable), the balance yet owed must be paid in full. It's expected that you'll be able to get a conventional mortgage at that time in order to pay off the seller.

Your goal is to achieve the longest balloon period possible, and never one shorter than three years. A longer balloon period allows you greater flexibility in terms of refinancing, selling, and judging the movement of interest rates. You obviously have more control over your investment when you have the time to decide when it's best for you to refinance or pay off the balance of the note. No matter what your balloon period, you should include in the contract some extension clause should you be unable to refinance at the end of the original term. (See our chapter on contracts for details.)

Why should you even consider a balloon payment?

Let's suppose you found a super buy on a 12-unit building, with super terms, as follows:

- Purchase price: $330,000

- Down payment: $30,000 (less than 10 percent)

- Owner financed: 8 percent interest, 25-year amortization, 12-year balloon note. (Current rates are near 16 percent and require 25 percent down-payment.)

- Monthly mortgage payment: $2,316 (approximately)

At the end of one year, with 10 percent appreciation, the property is worth $363,000. (Currently, you must own the property for at least one year and a day to qualify for long-term capital gains.) Let's say you can sell it for $370,000 by offering the following terms to your buyer:

- Purchase price: $370,000

- Down payment: $40,000 (a little more than 10%)

- Owner-financed: 11 percent interest, 25-year amortization, 7-year balloon.

- Monthly mortgage payment: $3,237.30

- Your original mortgage payment: $2,316.00.

- Your profit: $921.30 per month, or $11,055.60 per year.

    Let's take a closer look at what you've accomplished:

- You have recovered your original $30,000 down payment with a $10,000 profit. (That's a 33⅓ percent return so far).

- You have had one year's worth of depreciation and tax deductions.

- You pay only capital gains on the profit and on that portion of the $11,055.60 payments that are made toward reduction of principal. (Remember, with capital gains you exclude 60 percent of profit and pay tax on only 40 percent).

- You'll be paid in full (seven-year balloon) at least four years before *your* 12-year balloon is due, allowing you time to repeat the process with a new piece of property.

Just imagine repeating the entire procedure (buy-fix-up-sell) on three or four properties in four to five years. That $30,000 original investment would also "balloon," allowing you to grow financially at a faster rate and to retire even sooner. You would be "pyramiding" your original $30,000 into financial independence.

PYRAMIDING EQUITY

But you don't have to sell that wonderful buy that you've fixed up. Let's assume you keep it, and after three years, assuming a 10 percent a year appreciation, it would be worth about $440,000. You have another option now: refinancing.

If you refinanced up to 80 percent of the new value, or $350,000, you would gain an immediate $20,000 cash profit tax-free (you don't pay taxes on a loan, only on a sale). You also would have had the advantages of the previous three years of depreciation, interest deductions, etc. But if you did refinance, you would lose that 8 percent interest rate. To avoid that, you have still another option: a second mortgage.

If you obtained a second mortgage of $50,000 at 14 percent interest (assuming interest rates on second mortgages have dropped), you could keep your 8 percent first mortgage (if you have the deed). Now you still own the property; still have its tax deductions; and your increased cash flow (from higher rents—lower expenses) should take care of your mortgage payments on both loans. And—you now have $50,000 to invest in another property. You have *pyramided* your equity.

If you continue to own the property, you would eventually have to get a mortgage in the twelfth year to pay off the original seller. Actually, it isn't wise to hold property that long, from an investment point of view, unless you have refinanced it or used the equity from it to invest in other properties. You would lose too much money because the cash flow would not continue to be offset by depreciation. (Details in chapter on taxes and depreciation.)

In either case—selling after one year or more—do not stretch your available funds too thin. By using maximum leverage (almost 100% Financing), cash flow will be tight the first year. You'll also be putting money into the building for cosmetic improvements as you plan to raise income and lower expenses. Therefore, you need to have a reserve available for emergencies. You must be able to maintain control throughout your investment period so that you don't get hurt and become a must-seller yourself.

SHRINKING THE DOWN PAYMENT

As we mentioned before, 100% Financing—all the money is borrowed—is an ultimate goal. (It also assumes you can keep up with the payments.) But that doesn't mean the owner will accept *no money down*, which is sometimes unrealistic. It does mean that it's possible to buy a building without putting any of *your* money down. (Or very little.) One method is to have the money credited to your account.

Where does the money come from? Prorations of security deposits, rents, and real estate taxes, deferred payments, and possibly borrowing some of the real estate agent's commission. Attorneys like to do all prorations as credits and debits to simplify matters at closing. Any monies credited to you reduce the amount you owe for the down payment, as follows:

1. Security Deposits:

In some states (your attorney should check) security deposits can be used as the buyer's down payment. Although the security deposits belong to the tenants, as spelled out in the leases, they are only returned when the tenant moves. (Check whether your city or state requires the landlord to pay interest on these deposits.)

Therefore, those monies can be credited to your account at the closing.

Let's suppose you were negotiating the purchase of a 20-unit building that had security deposits in the amount of $6,500. You could add a clause in your contract stating that those deposits shall be credited to buyer and used as buyer's down payment. You immediately need $6,500 less to buy that property. If a tenant moved, you would have to reimburse his security deposit. But usually you can find a suitable tenant to rent the unit first and you get the security deposit from the new tenant to give back to the old.

2. Rents:

You should always close on the first of the month so that the rents for the coming month are credited to your account, and thereby used as part of your down payment. (Rents are usually due on the fifth of the month.) *Do not agree to collect the rents yourself.* Why? Because you don't know which tenants are slow payers, or might not be paying their rent at all. If you aren't credited with the proper amount, you could have difficulty collecting. But if you are credited, and a tenant doesn't pay, or is slow paying, it's up to the former landlord to collect the rent that has already been included in the down payment.

Example: A student purchased a large building with one of the contract clauses calling for the seller to credit the buyer with the first month's rent towards his down payment. The seller didn't want to do it this way, saying, "Whatever rents come in from the tenants, I'll sign over to you." Fortunately, the buyer's lawyer persisted. The lawyer knew that notices couldn't be given to the tenants in time asking them to please forward their checks to a new address. The end result was that the seller gave the full rent credit to the buyer. After the closing, the buyer (student) ran into the seller who was at the building, who was collecting some rent that a tenant or two hadn't paid. If the amount hadn't been already credited, the buyer would have had to be the one chasing after the rent.

3. Real Estate Taxes:

In most states real estate taxes can be prorated and credited to the buyer's down payment. These taxes must be prorated to the date of closing even if the seller won't give you a credit. They are re-prorated afterwards when the final amount is known. First, do try to get the prorated amount as a credit for your down payment, or as a debit off the mortgage balance. If the seller refuses, then have the tax amount put in escrow (with an increased percentage to allow for a tax increase) so that you know it will be available when the tax bill comes due.

If the taxes are prorated to the date of closing and used as the buyer's down payment, the buyer will be responsible for the seller's portion of the taxes when they come due. But in the meantime, the buyer gets the credit at closing, which means less money needs to change hands. And the buyer has the use of that money interest-free, until the tax bill is due.

As you know, real estate taxes are paid in arrears—that is you paid your 1981 taxes in 1982, 1982 taxes in 1983 and so on. You should be setting aside one twelfth of your rent income each month in an interest-bearing account, to cover taxes when they come due. If you're supposed to pay this tax money to your bank or mortgagee each month, check on the possibility of paying the taxes yourself. Otherwise you're building up a tax fund in the bank and collecting no interest on it. If you have executed a contract sale and the seller is keeping his mortgage and paying his taxes directly to the bank, you won't be able to use the method described.

To show you how the tax proration works, let's say that you're buying the same 20-unit building, closing May 1, 1983, and the tax bill is $15,000. The first half of 1982 taxes, $7,500 (usually payments are not equal), was paid by the seller in April 1983. The seller still owes the second half of 1982 taxes, or $7,500, plus four months (January, February, March, and April) of 1983 taxes; a total of ten months. Assuming no tax increase, you could be credited with ten months, or $12,500 worth of the possible $15,000 tax bill. ($15,000 divided by 12 = $1,250 per month, times ten = $12,500.)

Realize that this tax credit is yours only temporarily. The second tax installment of 1982 is due August 1983, at which time you owe the seller's second half-year of taxes of $7,500. You have been able to set aside out of rents (May, June and July) only $3,750 (assuming $1,250 a month). Therefore, you will have to come up with $3,750 out of your own pocket unless your cash flow is great enough to cover it (or you have borrowed it, or you have arranged with the seller to defer payments for a few months so you could set aside this amount). Don't forget the balance of that tax credit—those four months of 1983 will have to be paid for in April 1984. Of course, you have eight months (August through March) to set aside a six month payment (January through June), so you shouldn't have any problem making future payments out of your rent collections.

Always check state and federal laws for any possible restrictions. Also note that the above example does not apply in every state and payment dates may vary.

4. Gas, Water, Electric Bills:

These items can also be prorated to the date of closing and credited to your down payment. When you close on the first of the month, the bills for the previous month have not yet been received or paid in some cases. The previous owner is, of course, responsible for those expenses. They can be estimated, if not already known, and considered part of your down payment account. Just make sure that when they come due, you have the money available to pay them. These amounts can be considered a short-term, interest-free loan.

5. Deferred Payments:

When you close on, or near to, the first of the month, your first payment on the building is usually due within 30 days. Your attorney can try to add a clause in your contract stating that the first payment shall begin 60 to 90 days after closing. Of course, you still owe the seller the payments for the first 30 or 60 days and they will be tacked on to the balloon mortgage note balance. But in the meantime you are getting the use of the rental income money in the very beginning when you most need it. Many students have used this method successfully.

6. Real Estate Commissions:

It is possible to borrow part of your down payment from the

real estate agent, who may be willing to loan (or give) you part of the commission he will receive from the sale of the property.

Real estate commissions usually work as follows:

If a 12-unit building sells for $300,000, and the commission rate is 6 percent, then the real estate commission is $18,000. Many agents are realtors, or members of a Multiple Listing Service (MLS), and cooperate with other realtors on sales. One office may list a property for sale, but another office may find the buyer. Therefore in a cooperative sale, two offices would split the $18,000, each receiving $9,000. This amount is then split again between the broker (office) and the sales person (either the listing sales person, or selling sales person). Each can receive as much as 50 percent or more, depending on their arrangements within their offices, so that the two sales persons may receive $4,500 each, and each office (broker) would receive $4,500 each.

If the listing salesperson also supplies the buyer of the property, the $18,000 stays in the office, and is split between the broker and salesperson—$9,000 each. In such a situation, you might be able to borrow $9,000 of the commission from that office. Remember—they already had agreed to cooperate on the sale with another broker and salesperson, and thereby accept $4,500. So, in order to make sure the sale goes through, they may be willing to accept just $4,500 now and loan you the other $4,500 they received from the seller. Many graduates of our seminars were able to borrow from the real estate agents without paying any interest over a period from three to five years.

A real estate agent will, of course, be more anxious to work with you during tough times or with hard-to-sell properties. If you give the agent a note, promising to pay the loan back, it is considered better than nothing. Incidentally, a good agent should be prized because he or she will save you time on finding buys and make you money.

Using the methods described above, the following example shows how much money might be credited to your down payment on a 12-unit building, sale price $300,000.

Gross income:	$42,000
Expenses:	12,000
Net income:	$30,000
Rents average $292 per unit	$ 3,504 per month
Security deposits $250 per unit	$ 3,000 per year
Taxes	$ 7,000 per year
Real estate commission	$ 9,000
Monies available to credit towards down payment:	$22,504

In the above example, we divided the gross income by 12 months to equal $3,504 income per month (that divided by 12 units comes to just under $292 per unit average).

We assumed the security deposits were not raised from $250 per unit when the rent was raised to $292. We require one and one half times the rent for security deposits, so if we owned this building the average security deposit would be $438. We also assumed that you, the buyer, would be responsible for the full amount of taxes and so credited. And we further assumed that the real estate listing agent would loan you half the commission, agreed to by the broker.

Using deferred payments for 90 days, another $7,008 becomes available temporarily as follows (first 30 days rent previously included):

$3,504 second 30 days rent (or 60 days)
$3,504 third 30 days rent (or 90 days)

These deferred payments can buy you time before the first mortgage payment is due, but at the closing only the previous total of $22,504 is actually available to put toward the down payment. If the seller wants $30,000 as his down payment (10 percent of purchase price), then you must come up with $7,500 in cash. You also need money for attorney's fees, closing costs, and an emergency reserve. To be safe, therefore, you should have $15,000 in cash in order to purchase the property as described above.

Of course you could borrow that $15,000, as explained later in the chapter. And then you would achieve 100% Financing!

To summarize the above transaction: You purchased a $300,000 building with about $15,000 in cash. You came up with a 10 percent down payment and obtained a mortgage of $270,000 at 9 percent interest. The net income is $30,000 a year, out of which you make payments of $2,265.84 a month or $27,190.08 a year. That leaves you a cash flow of $46.48 a month, or $557.76 a year. Even if you borrow the $15,000, your cash flow could cover some of that cost. And that $15,000 isn't all spent; part of it still exists as a reserve for emergencies. That cash flow is only *current income;* it should increase when you raise rents and/or lower expenses. If you then figure in depreciation, you might not even have to pay taxes on the current or improved income.

7. Closing Costs:

Closing costs include attorney fees, clearing title expenses, and bank charges. The seller usually pays the cost of clearing title which isn't very expensive. Both buyer and seller have attorney fees and should ask in advance how much they will be. It's also best to get the estimated cost in writing. The bank charges include a credit check and an appraisal fee, which can also be checked out ahead of time. Bank charges, called "points," are based on the amount of the mortgage and can be avoided when you buy directly from the seller. But to give you an idea: on a $300,000 mortgage, a charge of three points (3 percent) would be $9,000—just for giving you the loan.

8. Using the Seller's Equity:

As a last resort, if you are short of funds for a down payment, but have good credit, you can sometimes get the seller's permission to use his equity on the property in order to borrow the amount you need from the bank. This method assumes that the purchase is a contract sale, that the seller is holding the first mortgage and the deed. In such a situation, the seller may be willing to permit you to place a second mortgage on the property. He turns the deed over to you so that you can turn it over to the lending institution in order to borrow the amount needed. The second mortgager requires the deed in order to prevent the owner, or holder of the deed, from merrily remortgaging the property with several other lenders. You would then be responsible for the payments to the lender of the second mortgager. The seller is protected with the first mortgage which allows him to foreclose if you miss any payments to him.

You should limit the amount borrowed to the seller's actual cash needs, if possible, because the interest rates could be quite high. Let's assume that the building is valued at $280,000, and the seller has $280,000 worth of equity (no mortgage). He needs $20,000 cash, which you don't have. He allows you to borrow that $20,000 from a lending institution by giving his permission with the deed. You turn over the $20,000 to the seller, and make the payments to the lender. A seller might prefer this arrangement to one that gives the bank the first mortgage and the seller the second mortgage. So would the bank because the first mortgagee is in the best position.

As we said, this arrangement is not so readily accomplished, but it is an alternative when other methods fail.

LEASE PURCHASE

A lease purchase agreement is often confused with an option-to-buy agreement. They are actually two different types of transactions. With a lease purchase agreement you will lease the property for an agreed-upon period of time, at which point the purchase agreement goes into effect. An option-to-buy (explained later in the chapter) does not bind the renter who may choose not to exercise the option.

A lease purchase arrangement can come about when a seller is anxious to sell but having a difficult time due to a combination of factors, such as high interest rates for conventional mortgages, or a due-on-sale clause in the seller's mortgage. The former factor limits the number of buyers who can afford the property, and the latter rules out a contract sale in most cases. The seller is faced with either selling the property at a much reduced price or renting the property to tenants who may greatly damage the property. In other words, we have a motivated must-seller.

Such a situation is ideal for a lease purchase agreement. You will probably need a financial package and references to offer the seller so as not to appear only slightly better than a renter. The amount of the monthly payments can be negotiated and even formulated as if the seller were receiving 9 or 10 percent interest under a contract sale.

For instance, if such a seller wanted $60,000 for his home, you could probably purchase the property with no money down. You would draft an offer stating that you would pay $500 a month, for three years, under a lease purchase, with a percentage (one third) of that rent to be applied toward your down payment of $6,000 (10 percent). If you paid $6,000 a year in rent, and $2,000 a year was applied toward your down payment, in three years you would have applied $6,000. At the thirty seventh month the purchase agreement would go into effect and you would have to get a mortgage in the amount of $54,000 and pay the seller off in full.

What were the advantages?

You purchased the property with no money down (in fact, you began a forced savings plan). Had you been able to purchase the property on contract at 9 percent interest, your monthly payments would have been $453.60 per month, amortized over 25 years, and about $48 per month would have gone to reduce the principal. You would have had to put the $6,000 down immediately and had a mortgage balance of $54,000. After three years you would still have owed $52,000. After three years with the lease purchase, you owe $54,000 but you paid the $6,000 down payment over three years instead of in one lump sum. Of course, you would have had to negotiate with the seller to determine how much of your payment should be applied toward the purchase price.

Another point to note is that you probably wouldn't have paid the full $60,000 for the property had you been able to purchase it on contract. So the seller makes more money with the lease purchase, and therefore has motivation to enter into the agreement.

Furthermore, by the time your purchase agreement goes into effect, the property may well be worth more than the $60,000 price you agreed to pay. If there was a 10 percent per year appreciation, the property has increased in value almost $20,000.

Many lease purchase agreements permit the seller to sell their property without the due-on-sale clause becoming enforceable. The mortgage documents should be reviewed by your attorney in order to make sure that all liabilities are outlined and understood by you prior to using a lease-purchase agreement to circumvent a due-on-sale provision. Chances are that if the due-on-sale provision is weak to begin with, and if interest rates drop, a lease purchase agreement will work out fine—but let your attorney be the judge.

Realize also that you must exercise your purchase agreement at the time so stated, or you might be subject to a lawsuit. It's best to include an extension clause in your agreement just in case interest rates don't come down, or go up. The clause allows you additional time to exercise your purchase agreement. A lease purchase agreement, if structured properly, could work out well for both parties—100% Financing for the lessee-buyer with an eventual sale to the seller. A deal is always more satisfactory when both parties gain.

RENT-WITH-OPTION

Renting with an option to buy is similar to a lease purchase. The difference is that with a rent-option you are not committed to purchase the property and the selling price isn't set. It is advantageous for the buyer, who may not have sufficient funds for a down payment, or isn't sure he wants to own the property. It's advantageous for the seller who isn't sitting with an empty piece of property. (Further details in our chapter on selling tips).

Usually, you ask the seller to allow you to rent with an option-to-buy, and to allow a credit of your monthly rent to be put towards your down payment if and when you purchase. You may have to pay a higher price for the property in the future, should you decide to buy, but you are also free to not exercise your option. The seller has not locked in today's price for tomorrow's sale, but then doesn't have the certainty of a buyer, either.

Don't let high interest rates, or little savings, discourage you from investing in real estate. Given the variety of methods, you can see there is no one "right" way to finance your purchase of property. But there is one "ideal" way and that's the way that will give you the maximum leverage and profit. The seller is the key: find out what he wants; find a way to give it to him. Then find a way for him to give you what *you* need. Seller-financing, tailored to your situation, may well be the method to bring you closest to your goal of 100% Financing—and financial independence through real estate.

8
CONTRACTS
The Art of Reading and Writing Fine Print

8
CONTRACTS
The Art of Reading and Writing Fine Print

Now you know where to find the buys and the different types of financing and funds available. The time has come to prepare your offer. Up to this point in the investment process, you've taken on the entire responsibilty:

- You've reviewed the property's income and expense sheet and attempted to verify the facts.

- You've decided you can afford the property at a price around ten times the net income, at a certain interest rate under suitable terms.

- You have physically inspected the property, making note of those features in need of cosmetic repair and/or professional help, such as roofing inspector, service or heating and cooling company, appraiser, etc.

Your next job is to find a good attorney.

It's worth the trouble and time it takes to interview different attorneys (or those who have had experience with them) in order to choose the best person for your real estate transactions. You should ask the attorney, or whoever is recommending him or her, the following:

1. Does he/she have a solid background in real estate?

2. Does he/she own real estate?

3. What type of transactions has he/she successfully put together? (Any similar to yours?)

4. Has he/she successfully handled trades or does he know the components of a trade?

5. Can he/she explain some of the new tax changes that affect your investments?

6. What are his fees and how are they arrived at? Some lawyers charge a percentage of the sale involved; it varies between 1 and 3 percent of the entire price tag. (On a $300,000 building, a 3 percent charge would cost you $9,000.) If the lawyer charges by the hour, ask for an approximation of hours needed to close the deal. We prefer to pay by the hour.

7. Does he return your calls? That's a must and means good organization.

8. Can he give you some references? (Check them out.)

Remember, if your lawyer makes a mistake, or doesn't know real estate law, you are the one who will be called in by the I.R.S. You are the one who could lose thousands of dollars. Since his fee is tax deductible anyway, please don't buy real estate without the services of a good lawyer.

DUTIES OF THE ATTORNEY

You must also know the duties of a real estate attorney so that after you have chosen one, you can judge for yourself if he/she is doing all that is necessary. In order for an attorney to protect you, however, he needs your help. Remember, he hasn't seen the property and will not, in all likelihood, be negotiating your terms with the seller. (You or the real estate agent will do that as explained later.) You are asking your attorney for a legal opinion, on paper, that will protect you and make *all* parties happy. The first duty of an attorney should be to *not* wreck the deal. The others are:

- Prepare contract in legal form, such as Articles of Agreement for Warranty Deed, to protect your interests.

- Determine the best way for you to take ownership.

- Establish trust (if appropriate); set up escrow at title company.*

- Order title, preview and make opinion on title.*

- Do prorations on expenses and taxes, revenue stamps, etc.

- Inspect all leases and mortgage documents.

- Contact other party's attorney.

- Organize and establish working relation between parties.

- Set closing date.

- Handle closing with all necessary papers to be signed.

- After closing record documents and handle other necessary paper work.*

  *Some additional fees may be charged for some of these needed services. Do get a list ahead of time of all the duties your attorney will be responsible for and the fees to be charged to handle your transaction.

Your attorney can also handle protestation of taxes, if you wish to try to lower the taxes, and can appeal for a zoning change if that is necessary.

Many times the mortgage lender instead of the attorney will call down title on the property. Even then, it's important to have the title policy reviewed by your attorney to protect your interest in the property.

As we stated earlier, in most cases your attorney handles the legal work, but not the actual negotiations. Your real estate agent usually negotiates the transactions, or if you—as seller or buyer—are working alone, then you will handle the negotiations yourself. A good real estate agent can be quite helpful when discharging the following duties:

- Provide information about current market conditions

- Be knowledgeable about types of financing

- Qualify the buyer

- Present any and all written offers

- Represent all known facts to all parties involved

- Order survey on property

- Negotiate the terms of the contract, including financing, date of possession, etc.

- Follow up with attorneys by supplying needed information and materials or documents
- Organize total transaction to closing

WHAT A REAL ESTATE AGENT SHOULD AND SHOULD NOT DO

Real estate agents *should not* tell you that you don't need an attorney. Agents are required to fill in the blanks of a standard real estate sales contract. They are *not allowed* to add any additional terms to the contract, even if their client requests it. In other words, they cannot practice law. If you wish to add protection to your contract (as we advise later), you as the buyer or seller may do so. Or, as we recommend, have an attorney do it.

If you wish to have an offer presented to a seller by a real estate agent, the offer must be in writing before the agent is required to present it. Should an agent refuse to present your written offer to the seller for whatever reason (low price, terms not in line with seller's wishes, etc.) advise the agent that he must do so by law in most states. (An attorney can advise you on the laws of your state.) If the agent still refuses to accept your written offer then ask to see his real estate license. Get the number and advise him/her that you will turn him in to the real estate licensing board. The real estate agent shouldn't make decisions for the seller. In many cases we have seen deals go through after the agent first refused to present the offer. Try to be firm but tactful. You don't want to create a hostile agent. You need the agent to work for you. Continue to present your good intentions toward the potential purchase to reassure the agent that you aren't behaving in an arbitrary fashion.

All attorneys and real estate agents are licensed in the state in which they do business. This license allows them to represent the public and make a living. They also have set up disciplinary agencies within their groups or organizations. As with any business, the majority are good but a bad apple can appear. If you should run across such a person, whether he be an accountant, attorney, or real estate agent, don't rely on the next guy to see that the proper agency hears about improper behavior or service. All the good, hard-working professionals need your help and support to rid their industries of those who misuse the public's trust.

WHAT IS A CONTRACT?

Legally, a contract requires six components:

1. The parties involved must be mentally competent.
2. The terms of the contract must be clearly understood by all parties involved.
3. It must be in writing and signed by all parties involved, partners, spouses, corporate officers, etc., as a voluntary act by the parties.
4. It cannot call for some illegal act to occur.
5. It must include a legal description as well as an address, and other type of description of the property.
6. The price or consideration must be stated in the terms, and some consideration, money or a promissory note, must accompany it.

For *earnest money* (the consideration that accompanies the contract) try to use only promissory notes. They are legal documents that promise to pay the stated amount on demand or on a specified date, and they cannot be cashed except as noted. Naturally such a note is to be preferred by the buyer because you don't have to come up with a check or cash at the moment. If you have to put up earnest money in cash, we suggest that you give it to your own attorney who will put it in an escrow account. Some real estate companies and sellers have been known to keep the earnest money and the buyers have had to go to great lengths to get it back. It's a shame to have to warn you, but we have good and bad people in all professions.

IS AN OFFER A CONTRACT?

Many people confuse the term "offer" as it applies to a contract. They think of it as a first, but not final step. That is not necessarily true. Whenever you sign a standard real estate contract form, or in any other way put terms together on paper, date, sign, and deliver these terms, with a consideration, to the propsective buyer or seller, you have just presented a contract (or an offer) to buy the property.

If the seller or buyer should also sign that paper, or contract, and if you haven't included any additional terms (or what we call "out clauses") then you have completed the sale or purchase of a property. That's it. Unfortunately, what you *didn't* put in could hurt you worse than what you did. If it seems we're trying to scare you, we are only doing so to reinforce the respect you need to bring to any "offer" or contract.

If you were to prepare a contract, and have it presented to the other party, and should that party change any word, it then would be considered a counter-offer, or, in effect, a new contract. Your first offer would therefore be voidable by you.

Note: Any change made on a contract, standard form or otherwise, becomes a counter-offer and is voidable.

For example, if a real estate agent presented your offer to the seller who made only one change—let's say on the price—the agent would then either bring the contract back to you, or advise you of the change. You then have three choices:

1. You can re-counter the seller's change in price and offer a new one—in effect a new contract.

2. You may accept the seller's changes and so indicate by signing your initials to the change. Now the contract is final (unless you still have some out-clauses to be satisfied).

3. You may walk away from the deal. If you choose this action, it's advisable that you deliver to the seller or agent a letter of your intention not to pursue the transaction any further.

TYPES OF CONTRACTS

There are several types of contracts and we recommend that you pick up as many of the standard forms as are available in your area. The more contracts you're able to review, the better acquainted you'll be with any unusual terms or language that might be inserted in the standard forms by the other party; and the better you can provide for your own protection in the contract.

A standard contract form will usually have all the necessary elements that make up a contract, along with the language necessary to protect both parties. For any additional protection, you must rely on additional clauses that you add or are added by your attorney. To that end, check with your attorney for a copy of any form he might use.

Some standard forms we recommend for study are:

- Chicago Title & Trust Form Contracts
  Form A—Residential; Form B—Commercial;
  Form C—Condominium
- Cole Legal Forms No. 74 Installment Agreement for Warranty Deed
- Pioneer Title, and other title companies in your area
- Local forms used by real estate agencies in your state
- Local forms found in your local stationary store

We use any of the following contract methods when we buy real estate:

- The Attorney-Drafted contract (with added protection depending on the specific property)
- The Standard Contract (with added "out-clauses," as seen at the end of this chapter)
- Letter of Intent

CHECKLIST FOR CONTRACT

When making your offer, or discussing it with your attorney, the following checklist can be used:

1. Price
2. Earnest money
3. Down payment
4. Interest
5. Number of years on mortgage
6. Balloon payment
7. Security deposits
8. Rent roll (tied to closing date)
9. Real estate taxes

10. Date of first payment

11. Leases

12. Discounting paper

13. Closing costs

14. Total amount of dollars paid to seller on fulfillment of contract (an impressive and reassuring number to seller who is financing mortgage)

15. Possible seller refinancing for 100% Financing

16. Have all the seller's mortgage documents checked to see if a due-on-sale clause exits.

THE QUICKER CONTRACT

Many people won't allow a contract to be presented unless it is first prepared by their attorney. This is the best method for maximum protection, if you have enough time and money to follow it. But here is what could and sometimes does happen:

Buyer A is very interested in the home of Seller Sam listed with a real estate agent. The home is desirable, and because of the tight money market the owner is agreeable to financing the property to assure a quick sale. Buyer A shuns the real estate agent's advice to prepare an offer, choosing to meet with her attorney first.

Buyer A sets up a meeting with her attorney and gives all the information necessary for the attorney to prepare a contract. Many attorneys will take this information over the phone and have the contracts prepared within a day. Let's say it takes two days to prepare this contract.

Three days after showing the property to Buyer A, the agent receives her contract. The agent now makes an appointment with the owner to present the contract.

Seller Sam asks to take the contract to his attorney before he will sign it. Another one or two days go by as the attorney for Seller Sam makes some changes. It then goes back to the agent who returns it to Buyer A who takes it back to her attorney to review the changes made by Seller Sam's attorney.

Meanwhile, back at the property, the agent is showing it to other buyers and another contract is presented by Buyer B to Seller Sam. Seller Sam likes the terms and agrees to the new contract because Buyer A has not yet signed and returned a counter-offer.

End result: Seller Sam has a sale. Buyer B has a house. Buyer A has attorney bills.

Although it may seem that we are ignoring our own advice about checking with an attorney, we would rather approach a purchase this way: allow the agent to prepare the standard contract (or prepare it ourselves). But put in a few out-clauses (see examples at the end of chapter) so we can walk away from the purchase if we so wish. Our purpose is to first get most of the basic terms agreed upon by both parties. Once the price and other terms are settled, we then take it to our attorney to add other terms and legal language to the contract. We still might lose the property if the additional terms cannot be agreed upon; but we don't have to worry about losing the property to someone else.

Once we get some of the most important parts of the contract in agreement, we are reassuring the seller that in all likelihood we have a deal and the contract now goes to our attorneys only to protect both of us. You can be sure that if you have the price and some other terms settled, the seller will be anxious to have the deal go through.

Once our attorney has the contract, we will outline how and where we need additional protection. Some information may still be forthcoming, such as results of an inspection, verification of expenses, etc. Usually we insert a great many clauses knowing that negotiating is a game of give-and-take. We don't expect to get all our terms, and so we will be ready to concede some to get others. We often add clauses that protect the seller, thus showing that we're not out to hurt or be hurt.

LETTER OF INTENT

We have often used a letter of intent to purchase to get the terms of a possible contract outlined and agreed upon by the seller and buyer prior to a formal contract being drafted. With a letter of intent neither you nor the seller are bound to any of the terms that you're trying to agree on. But once you come to an agreement with the letter of intent, those terms are usually included in the contract.

Larger properties often fall into a letter of intent approach because of the complexity and possible counter offers and recounter offers. Most real estate agents will present the letter of intent to purchase, but they are not bound to.

The key element that makes a letter of intent to purchase different from a contract is a *disclaimer clause* which states that the terms are not binding to either party and are subject to a formal contract being drafted and accepted by both parties. During this preliminary stage, attorney fees usually are not incurred.

You might write many letters of intent on different properties until one clicks—then spend your efforts on the main one or two properties. Remember, you need only one or two good buys a year to achieve your goal of financial independence.

LETTER OF INTENT TO PURCHASE

RE: Property location
    City, State
    Type of building

Pursuant to the sale of _____unit brick building

located at _____Chicago,

Illinois, this letter of intent to purchase includes the following terms on behalf of Mr. & Mrs. _____.

1. Purchase price _____

2. Down payment _____

Balance to be paid with monthly installments.

3. Articles of Agreement for Warranty Deed:

    $_____at a rate of

    _____% interest amortized over 29 years, with a balloon payment within three to seven years. Monthly payments shall be at $_____which includes principal and interest.

4.   Other terms: Deed shall be deposited into a trust account.

This is a letter of intent to purchase and not a formal purchase contract. Any further proceedings are dependent upon both parties ability to reach a contractual agreement acceptable to both parties and their attorneys. Formal contract, if any, shall be drafted within ten days after acceptance of general terms of the letter of intent which shall be used only as a guideline of possible terms. Nothing contained herein shall find either party bound to the purchase or sale of the building, since the parties acknowledge further negotiations are necessary.

Date:_____

Purchasers: _____

Sellers: _____

ESCROW CLOSINGS

An escrow is another way of saying a third party. With an escrow closing, which differs from state to state, an escrow agent (third party) handles the details of the closing. The agent could be the title company, real estate escrow company, attorney, trust or escrow department of a bank.

Usually your attorney will include in the contract all the necessary language and information for the setting up of an escrow procedure. Once the contracts are signed (and a separate escrow agreement, if necessary), all necessary documents are sent to the escrow agent to prepare for the closing. Unlike a typical real estate closing which has all parties or agents for the parties present to sign and exchange paper and money, the escrow agent handles all the necessary work orders, title checks, prorations, computations, payouts, and proper recordings of documents. (Nevertheless, *you* should always check on whoever is handling the recording of your papers.)

If for some reason the escrow agent doesn't get the proper and necessary documents and funds from either party within the time outlined, then the party who failed to do so could be considered in default and lose the down payment or be exposed to legal action.

The escrow account for closing is paid for by both buyer and seller and is an efficient and convenient way to handle a purchase or exchange of property.

OUT-CLAUSES

We couldn't possibly list all the potential clauses to cover every real estate investment situation. We, therefore, have chosen to list the most important types of clauses that are useful in most situations. You and your attorney will have to decide which to apply to a particular contract, and whether you need to add others as well. To aid you in these choices, we will give you the reasons behind those clauses we've included. Remember that the main purpose of any clause is *protection*. You need immediate protection—so that you can get out of a contract that doesn't have all the answers and verifications you need to make an informed purchase. And you need long-term protection so that you don't become a must-seller because of unforeseen circumstances.

1. Your simplest clause makes the contract subject to your attorney's approval of the contract. Then, if you've slipped up in negotiating terms, your attorney can simply not approve.

2. If you plan an installment purchase, you could make the contract subject to your attorney drafting the Articles of Agreement for Warranty Deed. Then any clauses included in that contract would be subject to your approval.

3. The contract should be subject to your attorney's inspection and approval of all mortgage documents. Your attorney will be looking for possible due-on-sale clauses, mortgage assumption or second mortgage possibilities.

4. The contract should allow you to inspect and approve all the

leases. It's very important that you also insist that no new leases be given out, or old leases renewed between the time the contract is written and the closing—without your approval.

5. Your attorney shall provide for all prorations. You want to get all the credits you can as you may need them for part of your down payment. (Check local laws to be sure they don't restrict you from using these monies as your credits.)

6. You need a clause that makes the contract subject to your inspection and approval of all the units of the building. It's best to avoid naming a certain date or deadline for such inspection. You should also have a number of days after the inspection to respond to what you've found. You could then decide you didn't like what you saw, or you could ask the seller to set aside funds for repair, or to do the repairs first. The repairs would also be subject to a new inspection.

You might not know anything about the mechanics of a building—the heating and cooling systems, water heater, roof, porches, structure, etc. During your initial inspection you may see something that looks in need of repair or replacement, or a tenant might mention that something doesn't work right. In such cases you'll need to call in a professional. You could then make your contract subject to an inspection of the roof, and if it's determined that the roof is in need of repair or replacement, the owner shall be liable for such repair or replacement.

The inspection clause is necessary even if the owner claims the property is in good shape. If the seller doesn't want to sign contract with this clause in it, ask what they are trying to hide.

7. You might consider a clause that allows you to re-inspect the property prior to closing. This is often called a final inspection. The cliche better-safe-than-sorry wasn't invented by real estate investors, but it well could have been.

8. You might need a provision asking for an escrow account to be opened at closing. Such a clause gives you time to make sure that all personal property that remained with the building is in working order—such as washers and dryers, stoves, ovens,

refrigerators, dishwashers, garbage disposals, air conditioners, etc. With such a clause you want a certain amount of money placed into the escrow account to provide protection in case any of the above aren't working.

9. One of the most important clauses provides for verifications of all income and expenses prior to closing. If any discrepancies are found, you have the right to void the contract.

10. When you did your original inspection, you should have checked the local building division to get a list of all the local requirements so that you will know if the property is in violation or not. If you're considering condominium conversion, you should have found out if there are any restrictions. If you are uncertain about any building code violations, then you need a clause to provide some protection should a violation become known after closing.

11. You might consider making your contract subject to an appraisal of the property. Why not? The banks won't lend money unless the property is worth the price.

12. An extension clause is vital if your contract includes any kind of balloon note. Anything can happen in the future with interest rates or your personal situation. Usually a seller will cooperate if you offer to increase the interest rate a percent or two for the extended period of time. The increased percentage is an incentive for the seller to possibly even double the time originally granted. The seller might wish to protect his future by asking for a floor to a new interest rate that may be tied to an independent index. For instance, if an extra five years is allowed, but at 2 to 4 percent below prime, the seller may wish to be assured that he won't receive less than his original rate should the prime rate fall.

13. A discount clause allows you to lower the balance owed on the mortgage if worded properly. Let's say that the seller wants a shorter term balloon period than you do. Your clause allows you to pay him off in that shorter term, if he agrees to a reduced price—a discount. Your motivation will be the savings from a lower purchase price. The seller receives an earlier cash-out payment. For instance if you had a $440,000 owner financed mort-

gage with a 7 year balloon and the seller really wanted to get a 3 year balloon you might state that should you (the buyer) pay the seller $400,000 within 3 years plus all interest for that period of time, the mortgage will be marked paid in full. You have saved almost $40,000—or discounted the note.

Let's say you're a little bewildered by all these clauses, and those you haven't even heard of. Why not buy an hour of your attorney's time so you can explain the particulars of your purchase—what you want to accomplish—and ask his/her advice on the legality and protection needed. As we said, every property may need special provisions to protect you. The clauses we've suggested should help you get started.

9
NEGOTIATING
A Game of Give and Get

9
NEGOTIATING
A Game of Give and Get

The key to successful negotiations is knowledge and patience. The more you know about the seller's needs, the better prepared you are to satisfy those needs along with your own. Negotiating is a game of give and get—give the seller what he most wants and get what you need. Knowledge means being aware of financing alternatives so you are not limited in methods to work out the transaction.

You need patience because time may be needed for your ideas to take effect after their presentation. Make the best possible offer, and if no agreement seems possible at the time, it may be that the seller just needs a few extra weeks to see things your way. After all, any offer is bound to have some surprises for the seller. Many a deal has been made weeks and even months after it was first negotiated.

If you finally exhaust all your options, and still cannot satisfy the seller, you might do well to record all the avenues you tried and how comfortable you felt with the negotiating points you made. Even when you have to walk away from a deal, you can still learn from the experience.

The following example of an actual negotiation will take you through some of the steps involved in the sale of a property made through Kevin Vaughan's real estate experiences.

The basic facts: The seller was asking $325,000 for his 12-unit building, 30 percent down ($97,500), and offered no owner financing, although he would consider it. The financial sheet showed the property's gross income was over $45,000 before expenses. The expenses of the property, including taxes and insurance, came to around $15,000. The net income, or cash flow, was $30,000—all based on the liar sheet. Compared to financial sheets of other buildings, the figures didn't seem much out of line. The buyers had about $30,000 to invest which amounted to 9.23 percent of the asking price.

The buyers and I (K.V.) agreed that we would not insult the

seller by starting with too low an offer. Therefore, our original offer was for $279,000, with $25,000 down, at 10½ percent interest, amortized over 29 years, with no mention of a balloon payment. The mortgage of $254,000, would work out to payments of $2,336.80 per month, or $28,041.60 per year. Returning to the seller's figures, his $45,000 gross, and $30,000 net income or cash flow, meant that the buyers would still have $1,958.40 left over for *their* cash flow. ($30,000 minus $28,041.60.) By putting $25,000 down, they would then be earning 7.83 percent return on that cash investment. We didn't expect the first offer to be accepted, but we had to start somewhere.

We then ran an amortization schedule showing the amount of principal and interest that the seller would receive—$813,206.40 at the end of 29 years. We used the total to point out the tax consequences and profit that would accrue to the seller.

We were unable to find out all we needed to know about the seller from the liar sheet, nor from the other agent, so our offer was actually a preliminary offer with many out-clauses for protection. I hoped that at the time of the presentation of the contract, to take place at the seller's building, which was also his home, that I would find out the details we had to know, such as:

- Why is the owner selling?

- Where is the current mortgage(s) held, if any?

- At what interest rate is the current mortgage, if any?

- Is the mortgage assumable?

- Does the institution holding the mortgage allow seller refinancing or second mortgages? Or is there a due-on-sale clause that might prohibit a contract sale.

- What is the seller planning to do with the proceeds of the sale, or the balance of the down payment, after closing?

The meeting was set and the listing sales person and I met with the seller. One of the first questions I asked the seller, to check previous information, was why he and his wife were selling. The answer didn't come as a surprise. He said that it was bad enough that he lived in the building, and had calls at all hours of the day to fix small problems, such as water drips, adjust windows during season changes, and listen to stories and complaints, but the complaints were affecting the life of his family. He pointed out that the tenants could have handled many of these problems themselves if he didn't live on the premises.

As his story continued, he told of the final straw. Two of his tenants had gotten into an argument, and he had been called by other tenants to break it up. Guess who got punched. It was obvious to us. His eye was still black and blue. Then worst of all, he said, he had to have them arrested and press charges, and now there was no more peace in the building. He wanted to sell and get out of a bad situation.

Then I asked why he was asking for a conventional purchase or financing arrangment.

He said he wanted to move and to buy a house in the same area.

Now we were getting somewhere. I then asked the following questions:

1. What area was he looking at for his new house?

2. What were the prices of the houses in that area?

3. Was he going to pay cash for the house?

4. If not, how was he planning to finance the new house?

5. What was he going to do with the balance?

His answers were:

1. He wanted to live in the same area as the location of his building because he liked the area and his children were in school there and he didn't want to uproot them in mid-year. He had other friends and family in the area, and his business was also located there.

2. He was looking at homes in the price range of $60,000 to $100,000.

3. He wasn't planning to pay cash for the new house, but was hoping for *possible owner financing on his purchase at below market rates.* But he didn't really understand owner financing and how it operated at both ends—seller and buyer.

The other agent and I then explained owner-financing to him, using his building as an example. We pointed out to him that if he sold his building with a conventional mortgage, the balance of his money would go into a bank and receive whatever interest rate then current.

Then we pointed out how his capital gains taxes would possibly be higher on a conventional cash sale compared to the capital gains tax that he would pay if he took his profit in installments. We, of course, reminded him that a cash sale was almost impossible to get because of current high interest rates, the high down payment required to qualify for a loan, plus the expense of loan points.

Knowing his situation now, we showed him that he could purchase his new home the same way that he might sell his old. That the low down payment, plus interest payments he would receive for his building would pay for most or all of his new mortgage payments.

He had purchased the apartment building several years earlier for $190,000 with $40,000 down, and a $150,000 mortgage at 8½ percent interest, with a 30 year amortization. His payments of principal and interest were around $1,153.38 per month, or $13,840.56 per year.

The building that he might buy would be in the range of $80,000, asking a $15,000 down payment (18.75 percent), and leaving a mortgage balance of $65,000, amortized over 30 years at 10 percent interest, requiring payments of $570.43 per month, or $6,845.16 per year, not including taxes and insurance.

If the seller accepted our offer of $25,000 down, and monthly payments of $2,336.80 per month, or $28,041.60, it would work out as follows:

Seller's current payments: $13,840.56 per year
Estimated payments on new home: 6,845.16
    Total mortgage costs: 20,685.72 per year
Estimated taxes and insurance on house: 2,000.00
    Total outlay: 22,685.72
Buyers payments to seller: 28,041.60
Less above estimates of first mortgage
and new house costs: 22,685.72
Seller's yearly profit: $ 5,355.88
         or   446.32 per month

If the seller accepted our offer, he would have covered his down payment on the new house out of the down payment from the buyer.

I didn't mention the real estate commission, seller's closing costs on both transactions, because I knew we could work around those obstacles later. My main idea was to get the seller to accept the concept.

The seller was now convinced that he could work something out with the buyers, if they would consider a counter-offer of:

$315,000, with $65,000 down, at 11 percent interest, 29-year amortization and a three-year balloon (balance to be paid in full in three years).

What did this counter-offer mean to the buyer:

They would have a mortgage of $250,000 that would work out to monthly payments of $2,392.50 per month, or $28,710 per year. (That original $30,000 net income less $28,710 equals $1,290 per year cash flow for the buyer.)

That meant that their original 7.83 percent return on their investment, would drop to 1.98 percent (based on a $65,000 down payment), and they were asked to put over 20 percent down.

The seller's offer might be considered a waste of time under ordinary circumstances, but we knew he was a must-seller and would sell on contract. We also later pointed out to the seller that he wouldn't consider a return under 2 percent on *his* hard-earned money. After all, even if the first example worked out the seller originally put $40,000 down when he first purchased the building, and could stand to make $5,355.88 profit the first year. That's about a 13.4 percent return on the seller's original investment, not figuring that the seller will have all his house mortgage payments as well as insurance and taxes covered from the buyer's payments—which brings that figure up to over 30 percent return on his original investment.

While the return on the investment was important to the buyers, they also knew that the income on the property was somewhat below the market, although the asking price was on par with the market. The potential was great because the building was in a prime condominium area and was made of flexicore—one of the best types of construction.

After much figuring and discussion, the buyers and I came up with another counter offer as follows:

Price $300,000, with $30,000 down, leaving a $270,000 mortgage at 9 percent interest, 29-year amortization, with a seven-year balloon (balance to be paid in seven years). Their monthly payments would be $2,187.43 per month, or $26,249.18 per year, leaving an estimated cash flow of around $3,750.82 per year, or a 12.5 percent return on their cash investment.

I returned to the seller and went through the same steps, showing his profit and how it could work with taxes, etc. But now I added a new twist. If the seller continued to own the building, with its increased value, and increased net income, his depreciation was insufficient to shelter his profit. His mortgage payments were around $13,800 for principal and interest, yet the net income before mortgage payments was about $30,000, leaving over $16,000 profit, most of which his depreciation, based on the building's value when he bought it, couldn't cover. Besides, the seller was unable to use the new tax laws to his advantage.

His basis for depreciation was as follows:

Original purchase price:	$190,000	$190,000	
Land estimate 20%	x .20	– 38,000	land estimate
Land value estimate	$38,000	$152,000	building value
Basis for depreciation:	$152,000		

He probably used straight-line depreciation over 35 years, according to earlier tax regulations. The total depreciation per year might have been about $4,342.86; not much more would have been allowed even for accelerated depreciation of 125 percent at that time. (Taxes and depreciation explained in later chapter.)

I also pointed out that all of his mortgage payment wasn't deductible—only the interest portion, which I calculated as 90 percent. Therefore $1,380 of his $13,800 mortgage payment *wasn't* deductible.

I made the following breakdown:

$30,000	net income after expenses
– 13,840.56	mortgage payment (principal and interest)
16,159.44	profit
– 4,342.86	depreciation estimate
$11,816.58	taxable income based on tax bracket

Compare with buyer's payment to seller:

$26,249.18	(buyer's yearly payment)
– 13,840.56	seller's mortgage payment on 12-unit
*12,408.62	estimated profit to seller

*Numbers would be slightly different because principal and interest proportions weren't broken down; assuming, for example's sake, that payment is all interest.

$12,408.62	profit per year
− 6,845.16	estimated payments for seller's new house, again
5,563.46	assuming payment is all interest, as above
− 2,000.00	taxes and insurance estimate
$3,563.46	seller's possible taxable profit

Don't let the numbers obscure the point: when the seller of the 12-unit sells on contract, he is taxed on any down payment proportionate to his profit and tax bracket. The seller was saving money by taking on a new mortgage that was being paid for by the buyer of his 12-unit. Capital gains would apply only to one eleventh of the profit (he lived in one unit of a 12-unit building), so the seller was able to defer capital gains on his unit as long as he reinvested, or purchased another residence for $1 more than his unit sold for. Therefore, instead of a possible capital gains tax on $110,000 profit, it would be based on approximately $100,833. This is a rough estimate that doesn't take into consideration deductions allowed the seller of the 12-unit, such as closing costs, commissions, attorney fees, etc., which would lower the capital gains tax and doesn't include used depreciation that will be added back to profit, as explained in the tax and depreciation chapter.

The seller looked hard at the counter-offer because I told him that these figures were only estimates and should be checked by his attorney and accountant.

The seller finally made a counter offer of: $300,000 price, $35,000 down, 29 year amortization at 9½ percent interest, and a five-year balloon.

The buyers agreed to the $300,000 price, the 29-year amortization, the 9½ percent interest on the balance, but asked for $30,000 down, a five-year balloon with a five-year extension clause added in the articles of agreement (see example in contracts chapter). This new offer meant the following numbers to the buyer:

$2,286.90 payments of principal and interest per month

$27,442,80 per year to the seller

Subtracting that $27,442.80 from the $30,000 cash flow, left $2,557.20 estimated profit, or an 8.52 percent return on their investment.

The contract of course called for many other terms and provisions, some of which are found in most contracts. And the deal was consummated.

We could have tried many other variations if the above hadn't worked. For example, if the seller had stuck to the original demands of a large down payment, we might have asked him to refinance a small amount at a slightly higher interest rate:

$150,000	seller's original mortgage at 8½%
20,000	refinanced
170,000	new mortgage at 12% or
	$1,756.10 per month
	$21,073.20 per year

The purchase price could remain at $300,000

The seller would keep the $20,000 from refinancing his
                                      mortgage
    The buyer would give   _30,000_ down payment
    Total down payment   50,000

    The seller would need   250,000 mortgage balance
    Buyer will assume   170,000 new bank mortgage
    Seller will give
    second mortgage of $80,000 to buyer at 9%
                                648.80 per month
                               7785.60 per year

The buyer then will pay:

    21,073.20 first mortgage at bank
    +7,785.60 second mortgage payments to seller
    28,858.80 per year for both mortgages
               deducted from $30,000 cash flow
               leaves $1,141.20 cash flow for buyer

With this example the return on the buyer's investment would be about 3.8 percent. Cash flow would be minimal and risk heightened. Therefore the buyer should have a reserve of cash, if needed.

Realize that the seller is getting more than the buyer's $30,000 down because he will also keep the $20,000 borrowed on his refinanced mortgage. The buyer takes on its cost, in payments, thus reducing the amount of the second mortgage that the seller needs to hold. In this example, the bank mortgage is assumable, an important cog in the wheel of this deal.

Another alternative:

The seller agrees to sell on contract and take on a second mortgage (he keeps the deed and has no due-on-sale clause). The buyer then can wrap the old mortgage in the new, as follows:

$150,000 at 8½%   original first mortgage
  20,000 at 16%   seller's second mortgage from bank
  80,000 at 9%   third mortgage that seller
                       is financing for buyer

The yearly payments for the buyer work out as follows:

13,840.56   on the 8½% mortgage
 3,232.80   on the second 16% mortgage
 7,785.60   on the third 9% mortgage
24,858.96   yearly payment, deducted from
                 $30,000 cash flow, leaves $5,141.05
                 cash flow for buyer.

In this example, the return on investment would be 17.14 percent.

The seller has another alternative to the above example: take out the second mortgage before selling to get cash, and raise the buyer's interest rate thus making more money for himself.

The following negotiation deals with a situation that is ideal for the buyer with little or no money for a down payment:

The owner wished to sell a small commercial shopping center in a good location. He didn't have a mortgage on the property and was willing to finance a buyer. His three tenants were on triple-net leases—they paid for all expenses relating to the property, including heat, electricity, water, taxes, insurance and maintenance. They paid a total of $1,500 per month, or $18,000 per year gross and net.

(Because the seller paid out no expenses the net and gross income was the same.)

The seller was asking $130,000 with a 20 percent down payment ($26,000) amortized over 30 years with a three-year balloon note.

The buyer had no money for a down payment, but he knew the seller was anxious to sell and move out of state to a retirement community. The buyer created a package similar to the type we described in the financing chapter. He then offered a purchase price less than the seller's asking price. He also asked the seller to refinance the property for $40,000 at any bank of his choice. The seller would keep $30,000 of the borrowed money and allow the buyer to have the $10,000 balance for property improvements. The buyer would pay all points and closing costs on the entire transaction, and make the payments on the loan. Those payments, based on a $40,000 loan amortized over 30 years came to $506 per month for principal and interest, or $6,072 per year. The buyer also asked the seller to finance the balance owed on the purchase price with a five-year balloon, and to defer payments to the seller for one year after closing.

The seller finally agreed to a $120,000 purchase price, and to finance the balance of $90,000 ($120,000 minus the $30,000 he kept from the bank loan as a down payment) at 9½ percent interest amortized over 30 years with a five year balloon note. The payments on this second mortgage would be $762.30 per month, or $9,147.60 per year. The seller also agreed to defer payments for one year.

Why would the seller agree? Two main reasons: this was the only offer he received for his property; *and* the package and demeanor of the buyer gave him the reassurance he needed that the promised payments would be made. But the seller *also* got:

- The final purchase price close to his asking price.

- $30,000 cash from the closing, which came to 25 percent of the down payment, and $4,000 more than he originally asked for.

- Had he originally refinanced the property himself, he would have had to pay the closing costs that the buyer was now paying for.

- The $30,000 cash he received was more than his year's rental income of $18,000, so he could afford to defer any further payments for one year.

- Because that $30,000 cash was from a loan borrowed on his equity, he didn't owe any taxes on it. He will pay capital gains taxes on the portion that is profit only when he receives the balance owed him—in five years.

- He can retire out of state, as planned.

Because it takes two to make a deal, let's see what the buyer got:

- $10,000 cash at the closing—enough to pay closing costs and points with money left over for a reserve or whatever he needs.

- A deferment of payments on the second mortgage for the first year, so his only outlay that first year will be the payments on the $40,000 loan, or $6,072.00

- He will receive $18,000 in net income from the tenants the first year, minus the above loan payment, or $11,928.

- After the first year, without any rent increases, his cash flow, or profit, is $2,780.40. ($18,000 income less the cost of both mortgages which total $15,219.60).

- Depreciation on the property will shelter his cash flow and probably some of his ordinary income as well.

Now you know the ideal situation: Whenever a seller has a low mortgage or no mortgage he is in an ideal position to refinance his property in order to get a down payment, and can usually carry a second mortgage. The buyer might have been required to sign as a co-mortgager to give the seller added security. The result is the same: 100% Financing for maximum leverage and profit.

We would like to summarize the key negotiating aids as exemplified in the two previous examples:

Amortization schedule—the printed sheet showing the seller the total principal and interest he stands to receive, carries a far greater impact than words alone.

Package—the smaller the down payment, the more important it is for the buyer to present himself as a person in control of the financial situation. His package proves to the seller, as it would to a bank loan officer, that he is aware of all the numbers involved and is a reliable individual. (See the chapter on finances for details on creating a package.)

Educating the seller—while many sellers may be vaguely aware of owner-financing, they often don't realize the tax implications of their decisions. Their depreciation allowance may no longer shelter their profits, and they may stand to pay higher capital gains taxes if they accept a cash sale.

Seller-motivation—the buyer cannot successfully play with the numbers until he knows what the seller really wants.

Playing with the numbers—once the seller's needs are clear, and the cash flow verified, the numbers can be rearranged in numerous ways so that both parties benefit. The buyer must always keep in mind the return on investment which is tied to the down payment as well as the cash flow.

We didn't explore the psychological aspects of negotiating with a seller because a good real estate agent uses the proper techniques and can usually represent the buyer better than the buyer himself. (See how to find a good agent in the chapter on selling techniques.) A third party often prevents complications that may arise from the emotional involvement of the seller and buyer. If you are dealing with an owner who is selling his own property, you may be better off asking a real estate agent to represent you, as buyer, for a flat fee or percentage of the purchase price. You can also read some books on negotiating. Ultimately they make the same point: find out what the seller really wants (his rock-bottom price, cash need, or reason for selling), and try to give it to him. You will probably have to educate him to the advantages of your offer and reassure him of your reliability and sincerity.

And remember that the key to successful negotiations is knowledge and patience.

10
MANAGEMENT
The Art of Managing the Most Out of Your Property

10
MANAGEMENT
The Art of Managing the Most Out of Your Property

A good investment deserves good management. But we have found that when you let someone else handle your money, their math and yours do not always match. That doesn't mean you have to do all the work yourself. You should be out looking for more buys—where the *big* money is. But it means that unless you are in control at all times, you'll end up where *no* money is. Therefore, we recommend the following management safeguards and techniques that have worked for us.

INSURANCE

Don't ever own real estate for even one day without insurance coverage.
When buying a building, the first thing you must find out is:

- What company is insuring the building?
- What does the coverage include?
- What is the cost?
- When is the next payment due?
- Was the last payment paid?

Usually, you can take over the current insurance on a building without much increase in the rates. But do check with other companies for quotes because they can fluctuate from $1,000 to $4,000 for the same coverage.

Choose a company that pays its claims promptly. The bank will want their payments whether you are paid for your claim or not. (One individual lost everything because the insurance company awarded him only $40,000 for fire damage. In fact, it cost $225,000 to repair the damages. Although he sued, it will take him about five to seven years before he gets his day in court—and another penny. In the meantime, the insurance company will probaby use the funds they haven't yet paid out to invest in real estate.) You can check on insurance companies by inquiring at the Better Business Bureau. Ask friends about their experiences with insurance companies and the promptness of their claim payments, and ask other building owners their experiences, good or bad, with insurance companies.

Make sure you carry plenty of liability insurance on the building. $1,000,000 in liability insurance doesn't cost much more than $300,000 in liability insurance.

While brick buildings cost less to insure than frame buildings, the area a building is in plays an even greater part in the cost of insurance. If you buy a building in an area where there have been many fires in the past, the insurance will probably be very expensive. Ask several landlords in the area what they pay and with whom they have their insurance.

Carry separate insurance policies for the furnace or boiler. If you have a fire because of a fuel leak, you may find your regular policy will not cover the loss. Ask your insurance company if they will inspect the boiler once a year, or if you should have the state do it. Some insurance companies will do the inspection and send a report to the state for you.

Plan for your insurance coverage to start on the same day you close.

CUT REAL ESTATE TAXES

Many times the taxes are too high for the income collected. But if your taxes are less than 25 percent of the annual rental, you don't have much of a chance to lower them. Check with owners of similar property in the same area. If yours are lower, you might not wish to pay the expense of an attorney to protest your real estate taxes. You may wish to hire a tax consultant on a percentage basis. Some charge 25 per cent of the savings, or no charge if they cannot save you money. But the terms must be spelled out before you employ them. In either case, your attorney or consultant will need a copy of all the leases pertaining to the building.

HIRE AN INDEPENDENT CONTRACTOR

The best choice for managing your building is an independent contractor (IC) who lives in your building. Ideally choose a young couple where the mother stays home with a small child. They usually need the extra money you pay them and can divide the chores. The wife is home to take complaints from tenants (a bonus for you). She usually will clean halls, basements, washers and dryers. The husband will paint, cut grass, shovel walks, and repair miscellaneous items around the building.

Have your lawyer draw up a contract for them spelling out exactly what you want them to do and how much they will be paid. An independent contractor is liable for his own insurance should he get hurt working around your building; he is also responsible for his own income taxes, F.I.C.A., and state taxes. Offer to supply the paint (their choice of color) if they wish to paint their own apartment. (Labor is the biggest expense, and good relations make a big difference.)

Furnish your independent contractors with supplies that you obtain at wholesale prices. Keep the supplies in a basement locker so he can do his work without bothering you.

Also open an account at a hardware store for incidentals, but get an itemized list each month. Then check on what is being used. If your IC buys two water hoses, and your building needs only one, you know you have a problem to correct.

If a tenant has a complaint, see if the IC can first solve the problem. If he cannot, call in a professional in the field (electrician, etc.).

Never call the IC before going over. Drop by unannounced to see if the grass is cut or the laundry room clean.

Show appreciation for a job well-done, let your IC know that you care about the building.

Offer extra jobs to your IC and not to outsiders so he can earn extra money if he so wishes.

Always ask your IC if he needs anything in the way of supplies or help.

Insist employees be courteous to tenants and encourage good relations. The tenants pay the bills. Warn the IC not to get involved in disputes between tenants. Let police do the job if they are needed.

Let your IC show empty apartments and take credit application information. (See sample application below.) He can phone you the details and you can get the credit history. If it is acceptable, let your IC accept a check for rent and security deposit and sign a lease with the new tenant. As manager of your building, he can sign the lease for you, give one copy to the tenant and send you a copy with the check. Insist your IC accept only a check or money-order—no cash.

CREDIT APPLICATION

Name of Applicant: _____

Social Security #: _____

Address: _____

Telephone#:_____

Time at this address: _____

Previous address if at present less than 2 years: _____

Age: _____ Number of dependents: _____

Applicant employed by: _____

If self-employed show type or name of business: _____

Address: _____ City: _____ State: _____

How Long:

Years: _____ Months: _____ Position: _____ Monthly Income: _____

Previous employer and address or school attended if with present employer less than 3 years: _____

How long: _____ Position: _____

Bank references: _____

Bank name: _____ Bank address: _____

Checking acct. no.:_____ Savings acct. no.:_____

Credit references such as: Dept. stores, bank cards, loans, etc.

Company:_____ Acct. No.:_____

Company:_____ Acct. No.:_____

Spouse's full name: _____ Employed by: _____

How long: _____ Position: _____

Monthly income: _____ Soc. Sec. #: _____

Signature of applicant:_____

Date: _____

INCREASE INCOME—CUT EXPENSES

Remember: You raise the value of a building by cutting expenses and increasing income. First of all, by cutting expenses, you automatically increase income (or stem loss). And second, by improving your property you are able to raise rents and increase income again. Therefore, maintenance, improvements, and energy saving go hand-in-hand with rent and security deposit increases.

The outside appearance of a building is very important to maintaining full occupancy. Therefore, as soon as possible:

- Plant flower seeds, grass seeds, evergreens, trees and bushes around income properties.

- Paint all trim.

- Use blacktop sealer on parking spaces and mark off with yellow paint the parking space for each tenant. Number each space. (Saves hassles.)

- Clean basements and hallways thoroughly.

Save Energy and Save Dollars

- Replace showerheads and sink aerators with water-saving ones. Usually you will cut your water usage 50 per cent.

- Reduce your hot water tank temperature from 180 to 125 degrees.

- For dishwashers, the setting should be at least 145 degrees.

- Reduce the watt size of light bulbs in overly bright areas.

- Install low energy bulbs instead of common ones. They will provide the same amount of light and reduce electric usage at least 10 per cent.

- If you have a gas boiler for hot water heat, keep turning down the thermostat in the winter until the tenants complain, then turn it up 10 degrees.

- Repeat the above process with air conditioning, only reverse (or raise) the temperature settings.

- Always put a lock-box on the thermostat or your tenants will play with the controls.

• Replace missing or damaged storm windows and save 10 to 20 per cent of heating costs.

• Install six inches of insulation in your attics. In two years the savings on heating bills will pay the cost.

• Always check for leaky faucets. One water leak in your sink, tub, or piping will result in a water loss of approximately 50,000 gallons per year. A hot water leak also wastes electricity and gas. One hot water leak can cost you approximately $240 per year. When you multiply that by the number of leaks, you can easily see money "down the drain."

• Always use an electric timer for hallways and outside lights. They should be set to go on when it gets dark and off when the sun rises.

Remember that all improvements which cut down on energy use in investment properties are tax deductible.

In 1975 energy costs averaged 27 percent of the total operating costs for apartment buildings across the country. From 1973 to 1975, payroll costs went up about 15 percent, repairs went up about 26 per cent, while utilities increased 48 percent. Heating costs alone shot up 98 percent! And these items have been increasing ever since. So it's big dollars and good "cents" to shave those expenses. The following figures show exactly what savings those "shavings" can mean. And remember the rule: 10 times the net. When you cut expenses (or increase income) you increase the value of the building ten times. (Save $1,000—raise the value of the building $10,000.)

Cutting Expenses on a 12-Flat in 1980
(approximate figures)

Item	Cost & Labor per year	Savings per year	Increased Value
A. Water gaskets	$100.00	$300.00	$3,000
B. Water-saver shower heads	200.00	100.00	1,000
C. Reduce hot water temperature	None	150.00	1,500
D. Install hot-water circulating pump	350.00	100.00	1,000
E. Install low-flow aerators on kitchen faucets	50.00	100.00	1,000
F. Brick in toilet tank	30.00	80.00	800
G. Electric timers	150.00	200.00	2,000
H. Special electric bulbs	50.00	150.00	1,500
I. Door-closers	100.00	100.00	1,000
J. Adjust thermostats	None	300.00	3,000
K. More insulation in attic	300.00	300.00	3,000
L. Install missing storm windows	300.00	100.00	1,000
M. Clean furnace once a year	75.00	150.00	1,500
TOTAL	$1,705.00	$2,130.00	$21,300

RAISING RENTS

- Before you make out a new lease with a tenant, check your area for the average level of rents and make yours comparable. *Do not undercharge.*

- You can usually raise rents 8-15 percent a year, except in rent-controlled areas.

- Don't overlook late-charges (for tenants who pay their rent late).

- Make the security deposit equal to at least one and one half months rent.

   If you want to show appreciation for a good tenant, *Do not decrease rent nor withhold increase,* or you will deprive yourself of thousands of dollars in increased value and equity. Instead buy the tenant carpeting, or paint the apartment.

- Consider installing coin-operated washers and dryers.

- Consider constructing garages that can be rented out (one garage per three apartments).

- Charge for any damages to the apartment and give the money to your IC to restore apartment to suitable use.

   Let's take a quick look at what these few expense-cutting suggestions could do to the net—and your building's value:

   Three washers and three dryers for a 24-apartment building should bring in $10 per month per apartment, at a tax deductible cost of less than $2,000.

```
    24  apartments
  × 10  income
  $240  per month
  × 12  months
$2,880  per year net × ten = $28,800 increased value
```

One garage every three apartments, or eight garages, one stall, inexpensive, financed, tax deductible, rented for $25 to $35 per month.

---

8 garages
× 30 income

240 per month
× 12 months

$2,880 per year net × ten = $28,800 *increased value.*

Adding both laundry and garage incomes, makes $5,760 per year, and an *increase in value of* $57,600.

Let's now see what good management—in terms of increasing income—can do for you after one year:

In 1979 you paid $480,000 for a 24-flat with an income of $72,000 and expenses of $24,000.

You did your job and raised income through the various approaches, 20 per cent, or $14,400. New income now $86,400.

Then you lowered expenses 20 per cent, or $4,800.

Your new value would be: $14,400 times ten = $144,000
4,800 times ten =   48,800
Increase $192,000
Original value 480,000
New value $672,000

But rather than ask what you can now sell your building for, ask what kind of building can you now trade your equity for. A building at least in the price range of $2,400,000. This is what is known as pyramiding in real estate. And this is also why it is important to repeat the procedure—buy and trade—as often as possible. (See chapter on exchanges or trades.)

OWNER-MANAGER DUTIES

The owner-manager's duties fall into *general* and *daily* duties. Your general duties were incurred when you first bought the building. It included hiring the independent contractor; cutting expenses; raising income; checking insurance and real estate tax costs. Your daily duties are not necessarily done *every* day, but they are repetitive and relate primarily to tenants—their leases and the requirements thereof. Therefore, we suggest the following:

Rent a post office box near your home.

Don't collect your rents in person, but have them mailed to a post office box. The cost is reasonable, depending on the size of the box, and cuts down on complaints, while saving you the inconvenience of not finding a tenant at home. Along those same lines, don't let tenants know where you live.

Consider installing a separate phone whose number your tenants will have so that you know when a tenant is calling.

Join the credit bureau in your town. It costs between $50 and $75 a year to belong to a Credit Bureau. You can then check the credit on tenant applicants by phone for a reasonable fee ($2 to $3 per credit report). This fee is deductible or can be charged to the tenant-applicant. (See credit application form.)

Some applicants may not fill out the form because they know you'll find out about their failures to pay past creditors. (An applicant can look like a million bucks—because he rarely paid any creditors in the past).

When you tell tenants that you belong to a credit bureau, and that they may use you as a credit reference, it makes them more aware of their credit rating, and more timely with their rent payments.

PROVIDE IRON-CLAD LEASES

Leases differ across the country, and some states have approved leases that must be used. In your local stationery store you can buy some blank leases—specify apartment or commercial store leases. The standard lease covers owners quite well, but we believe in adding another page with the heading, "Rider to the Lease," which is to be dated and signed by both parties (owner and tenant).

Following are the covenants, or agreements, that should be in your lease and/or the rider to your lease:

1. Date of lease (it *must* be dated)

2. Term of lease (say 11-1-81 to 10-31-82). Usually the term is for a year because the future of inflation is too unpredictable. Or you can write a 2-year lease with a built-in increase of 10 percent the second year.

3. Amount of rent to be paid monthly—in advance until termination of lease

4. Amount of security deposit

   We like the security deposit to be greater than the amount of rent—usually one and one half or two times the rent. Security deposits do not earn interest unless and except as required by law. Also, upon termination of the lease as stated in the lease, the lessor (owner) may take monies from the security deposit to repair or replace any damaged property in the apartment. The lessor will provide to lessee (tenant) an itemized statement of cost of repairing or replacing damaged property. The security deposit may be used for any rent which is not collected by lessor.

5. Liability—lessor (owner) shall not be liable for any damages that arise from a failure in plumbing, gas, water, snow or ice (except as required by law). Nor any damages due to neglect by a co-tenant of the same building. Nor shall lessor be liable for theft of articles owned by lessee in the apartment or storage areas. (Advise tenants that insurance companies sell renter insurance at a reasonable price if they wish to have it.)

6. Sublet—Lessee (tenant) is not to sublet or use apartment for any unlawful use. It is not to be occupied by any other persons other than those first rented to unless so permitted by lessor. Lessee is not to use apartment for any business operation.

7. No pets. Lessor will not permit any pets or animals in building.

(I have found that animals will disturb other tenants and destroy property.)

8. Disturbances. Lessor will not permit any loud music from T.V., musical instruments, stereo, or personal noise that disturbs fellow tenants or violates any regulations or city ordinances.

9. Cleaning and painting charge. Lessee will pay for all cleaning and painting charges due to misuse. Lessee must return apartment in good order and condition as received. Lessee will be charged for cleaning dirty stove, refrigerator, carpeting, repainting of scratched walls, repairing of holes in walls, and/or cleaning any soiled area in apartment. (You might want to specify amount in dollars for cleaning such as:

   • Cleaning dirty stove—$25

   • Cleaning refrigerator—$25

   • Cleaning kitchen floors—$25

   • Cleaning carpeting—$90

   (You might also specify that if the apartment has to be painted because of writing on walls, scratches or holes in walls, the charge will be in the amount of the cost to do so.)

10. Late charges. Lessee will be charged $15 (except as required by law) in addition to rent, if rent is not paid when due. If late charge is not paid, it will be subtracted from security deposit at a later date. (Explain to tenant that if they pay on time they can use you as a credit reference. The majority will pay on time.)

11. Changes or alterations to apartment. No changes or alterations of the premises shall be made without lessor's permission. If lessee erected partitions, walls, wall-papered, installed doors or locks without consent, lessee will make all repairs necessary to walls, ceilings, doors, and paint in order to return apartment in same condition as lessee received it—or lessee must pay the cost to do so.

12. Access. Lessee will allow lessor access to the premises during reasonable hours in order to allow lessor to make repairs, improvements (as lessor may deem fit to make), and to sell the building, and lessee will not interfere.

13. Vacate. If lessee vacates apartment, lessor may rent the premises as he sees fit. Lessee is responsible for all deficiencies in rent because of lessee vacating premises and must pay lessor that amount owed.

14. Attorney's fee. Lessee must pay all attorney's fees and court costs to the lessor if the lessor has to enforce rights by lease or by law.

15. Restrictions. Lessee shall not install washers or dryers in the apartment. Lessee is not to leave articles in hallways of building. Lessee is not to install any type of antennaes on the outside of building.

16. Holding over. If lessee remains in possession of said premises after termination of lease, lessee has to negotiate a new lease with lessor or quit premises. For each month after termination of lease, lessee will pay double the rent in the terms of this lease. (I, personally, want a new lease with updated clauses and terms spelled out which is why I ask for double the rental.)

17. Water & Heat. Lessor shall provide hot and cold water at all fixtures for the use of lessee. (Again, lessor is not responsible during period of repairs.) Lessor will also supply heat from October 1st to April 30th in reasonable amounts when necessary, or by requirements of municipal ordinances. Lessor is not responsible during repairs or failures beyond lessor's control. (Note: You might want the lessee to furnish heat if building is so designed.)

18. Fire and casualty. In the case of fire or a casualty lessor may, at his option, terminate the lease or repair the premises within 30 days thereafter. If lessor completes the repairs in said time, lease will remain in effect. It is understood that if lessor does not complete repairs within 30 days, then the lease is terminated, but

lessee is still responsible for portion of rent due up to the day of such fire or casualty.

19. If any clause or portion of this lease shall be invalid or unenforceable under law, such clause or portion of this lease shall not affect or render invalid or make unenforceable the remainder of this lease.

While we suggest you use the standard lease sold in your area, and add to it those riders mentioned, we still would not recommend that you create an entire lease yourself, without an attorney's attention. Once your attorney has approved a lease, you can probably use it again with other properties. But it would still be a good idea to check again with your attorney just in case some new laws have been passed that could affect your lease provisions.

BOOKKEEPING

1. Open a separate checking account for *each* building with the address of that building on the check.

2. Deposit all income checks from one building through its own account and pay all expenses of that building from the same account. (This method satisfies many I.R.S. questions.)

3. Keep rental *income* records in a *green* notebook and rental *expenses* in a *red* notebook.

4. Make an income chart for each rental building. (See attached "green" chart.) Note:

   • The "green" chart shows who has paid and who has not.

   • You see at a glance when each lease expires and can send the renewal lease at the proper time.

   • You quickly see what security deposits should be increased.

   • You see who pays late charges too often. (If you wish to rid yourself of an unsatisfactory tenant, you might be able to greatly increase their rent when you renew the lease—unless your state has rent controls.)

5. Make an expense chart for each building as a double check (besides cancelled checks) so you don't forget to claim all your deductions on the I.R.S. forms. (See attached "red" chart). Note:

   • The "red" chart shows you graphically if electric, water, or gas suddenly jumps in cost. Then you can compare a January gas bill, etc. from one year with the January gas bill from the year before.

   • If the gas bill jumps, it may be that the thermostat on the furnace is set too high.

   • If the water bill suddenly doubles, the problem is several leaky water faucets or a broken water pipe.

   • If the electric bill zooms, check the timer and reset it.

   It will be well worth your effort to get used to recording and reading the following charts. They can keep management molehills from turning into mountains and keep you from turning into a must-seller.

(Red chart)

Expenses	Jan.	Feb.	Mar.	April	May	June	July	Aug.	Sept.	Oct.	Nov.	Dec.
Gas (heat)	$180	180	70	40	30	30						
Electric	40	40	40	40	90	90						
Water	60	-	60	-	135	-						
Taxes	$1,130											
Insurance	540											
Waste Disposal	40	40	40	40	40	40						
Supplies	150	-	200	-	-	100						
Repairs	Apt.#2 Z-Elec. $40	-	-	Apt.#4 Z-Elec. $40	-	-						
Misc.	-	-	Used Stove $170									

(Note: The electric bill rose in May and June because of air conditioning)

Address _____   Date _____

(Green chart)

1312 Kenmore 1981

Rental Amount	Name	Apt.#	Jan.	Feb.	Mar.	Apr.	May	June	July	Aug.	Sept.	Oct.	Nov.	Dec.	Security Deposit	Lease Expires
$220	Jones	1	220	235¹	220	220	220	¹							$190¹	7/31/81
$215	Smith Paul	2	215	215	215²	Vac.	245	245							360	4/30/82
$225	Olson	3	225	225	225	225	225³	225							200³	8/31/81³
$235	White	4	235	235	235	235⁴	235	235							235⁴	8/31/81⁴
$230	Young	5	230⁵	230	230	245	245	245	245						245⁵	3/31/82⁵
$225	Cassidy	6	225	225	225	225	225	225⁶							200⁶	9/30/81⁶

Notes:

1. Jones was charged a $15 late charge in February. He is late with the June rent, so I'll be looking for his late charge. His security deposit is less than the rental because the previous landlord didn't increase it when giving a new lease. When his lease expires in July, I will request an increase in the security deposit plus an increase in rental. The new rental will be $245, so I will ask that he pay $55 extra to bring up the security deposit. If he were to move, I would ask the new tenant for a security deposit of 1½ times the rental (about $360). Never accept a new tenant without rental and security deposit in advance.

2. Mr. Smith moved out March 31, 1983 and it took me a month to find a new tenant, Mr. Paul, who signed a lease at a rental of $30 more. Mr. Paul was my first tenant to pay the new increased security deposit of $360.

3. Mr. Olson's lease will expire August 31, 1983 and will receive a new lease, 60 days in advance, asking for $245 a month, with a note asking for $45 more for the security deposit. I send all leases out 60 days in advance and ask for them back in 30 days. That gives me a 30-day head-start in finding a new tenant.

4. Mr. White's lease also expires August 31, 1983 and he will also receive a new lease asking for $245 a month, with a note asking for $10 increase in the security deposit.

5. Ms. Young's lease expired March 31, 1983. She decided to stay another year with an increase in rental of $15 and the increased security deposit.

6. Mrs. Cassidy's lease expires September 30, 1983 and she will receive a new lease with a $20 increase in rent to $245, with a note asking for $45 more for the security deposit.

EVERYTHING YOU SHOULD KNOW ABOUT TENANTS

If you want to know what's going on in your building—ask a tenant. Tenants will tell you about:

- Miss Brown's male visitors

- When your independent contractor is working around the building—and when he is not

- The lower rents in the area (but not about the higher ones)

- Anything you care to know

Tenants will also test you by telling you things that are not necessarily so. They might say their rug is worn out. If you check it, it probably could last three more years. They might say the last landlord promised to paint their apartment within the next three months, right after you took possession. If you check the lease you might find that the apartment gets painted every three years and these tenants were in their apartment only eight months when they told you of the "promise."

Rent increases are rarely kept secret. If you raise one tenant's rent, you can be sure everyone in the building will know the amount of increase.

The "Rotten Apple"

Don't fool around with bad tenants. They usually instigate trouble and cause you nothing but problems. One way to get rid of such tenants is to tell them at the time their lease is up that they will have to move because of remodeling. Or, if there is no rent control in your community, raise their rent a substantial amount. Or, if you need to move tenants out as soon as possible, read over their lease and find something wrong so you can bring them to court, if necessary.

Don't get personally involved with wild parties or fights. Let the local police do their job.

And don't let these warnings discourage you, because you will find out, as we did, that the good tenants outweigh the bad.

MANAGEMENT COMPANIES

You can hire a management company to rent your building and/or to manage it. Their rates are negotiable and range from 5 to 10 percent of the gross annual rental the first year for renting a house, apartment building, office or store. They sometimes charge an additional 2 to 3 percent of the gross annual rental for the remaining years of a particular contract or lease. They usually charge about 5 percent of the rents collected to manage your property. Their fee can be paid monthly or annually. Their duties are as follows:

1. Collection of rents

    At the end of the month they give the owner a statement showing who has paid and who has not. They usually consult with tenants by phone and mail about late rents. The cost of any necessary legal action seems to rest on the owner's shoulders—it does not come out of the 5 percent management fee.

2. Attention to complaints and repairs.

    While they must satisfy tenant complaints and see to it that repairs are made, the costs of such repairs are paid by the owner—they do not come out of the 5 percent management fee. Such repairs could cover:

    a. Heating

    b. Electrical

    c. Carpet replacement

    d. Plumbing

    e. Glass/window replacement

    f. Stove and refrigerator repairs

    g. General wear and tear

A good management company ideally should be cost-minded. They will purchase supplies at cost or wholesale when needed. They usually pay all bills for labor and supplies out of the rents collected and note this in the statement the owner receives at the end of the month.

3. Fill vacancies

They take the responsibility for renting the apartments, offices or stores.

When choosing a management company, be very careful. Ask for references and check with some of the other landlords in the area before signing with any one company. Remember, they are handling your money.

Our experience has taught us that the other fellow doesn't seem to care the same way we do. Therefore we believe that the owner should handle the financial matters, if at all possible. If you are in control of your expenses and in control of your income, you are in control of your property. And control is the essence of good management.

11
EXCHANGES
OR TRADES
A Way Up the Pyramid

11

EXCHANGES OR TRADES
A Way Up the Pyramid

In some cases it is more advantageous to exchange investment real estate for other investment real estate rather than to sell your property first and then buy another. If handled properly, the benefits usually outweigh the effort involved. But most people avoid exchanges for the following reasons:

• Lack of knowledge.

• Lack of proper planning (they often act on impulse when the cash flow has increased greatly and the paper loss—depreciation—can no longer shelter the profits.)

• They have become must-sellers because of some personal problem.

None of these is a very good reason for turning your back on a method that could save you taxes and improve your real estate holdings significantly. If you trade "up", for instance (buy a higher priced property), you may be able to defer the capital gains tax until the time you sell the exchanged property. Remember, whenever you defer taxes you are getting a government loan interest free.

In order to decide whether a trade is to your advantage, and whether you can defer all or part of a gain on the original property, you must determine the current basis of your original property. In order to do this, add up the original cost of the property plus the legal and financial costs to acquire it; plus the cost of the added improvements. From this total, subtract the amount of the depreciation previously deducted. Second, add to this any cash paid out or any increases in mortgage debt between the two properties. Finally, subtract any cash received in the exchange and any decreases in mortgage debt. The result will be the new basis of the property. For example:

You want to trade your 6-unit for a 12-unit as follows:

	6-unit		**12-unit**
$165,000	current value	$350,000	current value
+ 75,000	used depreciation recaptured	– 140,000	profit deferred
$240,000		210,000	depreciation basis of property
– 100,000	orig. purchase price	– 50,000	land value
$140,000	profit less other deductions	$160,000	new depreciation basis of building

For tax purposes this will be treated as follows:

$100,000   Original cost of 6-unit including legal fees and original loan fees. This included $15,000 for the cost of the land.

(–)75,000   Depreciation of 6-unit deducted up until the date of exchange.

(+)185,000   Cash paid or mortgage taken representing the difference in current values of property.

($350,000 minus $165,000) including all fees paid in connection with the transfer.

$210,000   Tax basis of 12-unit property

(–)50,000   Land value of 12-unit (cannot be depreciated)

160,000   Basis for depreciating 12-unit building

Note that you have to subtract the amount of used depreciation on your 6-unit ($75,000) from the depreciation basis of the 12-unit

($300,000). You now begin depreciating the 12-unit starting from $160,000. You may now choose an entirely new method of depreciating this $160,000. You do not have any capital gains tax to pay on the profit from the sale of the 6-unit, if you also have adhered to the following requirements.

1. You must trade property for property without "boot" (cash or some other sort of compensation or net reduction in mortgages) in order for the exchange to be tax-free. Any gain in the form of "boot", or nondepreciable property such as land, will be taxed (explained below).

2. You must trade property of like kind, which refers to the nature or character of the property, not its grade, quality or use (an office building for an apartment building; or farm land for a city lot are examples of like kind).

3. The property traded must be held for productive use in your trade, business, or for investment and must be traded for such property. (Special rules apply to trading your home, to be discussed later.)

4. A person who is considered a dealer cannot have a tax-free exchange of property he holds for sale to customers.

5. You cannot deduct a loss in a tax-free exchange; to deduct a loss you would first have to sell the property, then buy a new one with the proceeds.

While you "lose" depreciation by trading, as opposed to selling and buying, the tax-deferred advantages usually outweigh the loss (the reduction of depreciation basis in new property). Therefore, if you wish to really grow in real estate holdings, trading can be one of your best aids. You should look ahead, however, and plan for the possibility.

Consider the following as soon as you purchase any piece of property:

- Plan on holding it for at least a year and a day to qualify for long term capital gains should you wish to sell it.

- If you wish to trade up, plan to do so within at least three years.

- Because of carry-over depreciation, be careful to pick the proper depreciation method.
- Raise income and lower expenses as quickly as possible in order to raise the value of your property and improve your selling or trading position.
- While you're raising the value of your property, begin looking for a possible trade.
- Calculate the amount of depreciation that you'll be using in order to determine how large a property you'll need in trade to make the deferred capital gains worthwhile.
- Before you make a final decision, determine whether you will gain or lose money by trading instead of selling and paying capital gains. This is especially important if you have owned property for some time. For example:

If you have used up 15 years of depreciation, totalling $160,000, you and your accountant must determine if it is feasible for you to look for a trade to defer a capital gains tax on that amount.

Another example: If you have owned your property for several years and it has appreciated greatly through improved income, inflation, and your mortgage reduction, it might be best to pyramid the amount of equity in the property rather than sell or trade it.

For instance, in the above example, I would prefer retaining ownership of the property and refinancing it—using the money to purchase other investment properties that would allow for exchanging within a couple of years. By refinancing, you pay no tax on the borrowed money; you can purchase more real estate for further sheltering of income and cash flow; possibly the cash flow on the properties will pay back the loan, the interest on which is also tax-deductible.

As you can see, you should never limit yourself to any one way to obtain results in real estate. If more people understood exchanging, however, more exchanges would take place. Some groups have been formed in cities to facilitate the exchange process, exchanging information as well as real estate.

TRADING FOR PROPERTY AND "BOOT"

When trading real estate you are trading equity for equity. But sometimes the equities are unequal. For instance, you may have $60,000 equity in your property, but the larger building may have an $80,000 equity. You have to make up that difference of $20,000. You have various options, such as:

- You can give cash, or a combination of cash and personal property, such as gold, diamonds, stocks, or a car, that carry the equivalent value. Of course, you'll probably have to provide an appraisal of the personal items to verify their true value.
- You can give the owner part cash and a note for the balance of the $20,000.

The amount of boot or amount given to match equities is subject to taxes to be paid by the person *receiving* the boot. You cannot claim a loss on a trade; the amount of any loss is added to your investment, increasing your total investment in the property. Note that the person paying the compensation is likely to receive the tax-deferred exchange, while the person receiving the compensation will have to pay a tax, if such compensation is in the form of boot or non-depreciable property such as land, and if the person receiving such boot has also realized a gain on the trade.

TRADING MORTGAGED PROPERTIES

If you trade mortgaged property for unmortgaged property, the mortgage released is treated as boot money received, even if the buyer assumes or takes property subject to the mortgage.

For example:

A owns 6-flat—fair market value:	$200,000
less mortgage of:	80,000
equity:	$120,000
B owns vacant multi-unit land (FMV):	$105,000
less mortgage of:	– 0
equity:	$105,000

"A" receives from "B" some cash and personal property worth $15,000 (the difference in equities). But "A" would also be released from the $80,000 mortgage, thus receiving a total boot of $95,000. All or part of that boot will be taxed depending on whether "A" realized a gain on the trade. When boot such as cash, personal property, or assumption of a mortgage is received, the owner cannot claim a loss or a deduction on his income tax. Rather, that loss is added to the new investment, increasing the total investment in the newly acquired property.

If both properties being exchanged have mortgages, the party giving up the larger mortgage and taking on the smaller mortgage must treat the excess as boot. In effect, mortgages are treated as cash. If the amount of the boot exceeds the amount of actual gain, then tax is limited to the amount of the gain.

For example: You own a small office building worth $250,000 with a $150,000 mortgage. Your equity is thus $100,000. Assume you had a remaining undepreciated basis of $175,000, you exchange it for a larger building worth $245,000 with a $145,000 assumable existing mortgage. There is no cash transfer since the equities are the same. Therefore:

Present value of the new building:	$245,000	
Mortgage assumed on new building:	– 145,000	
		$100,000
Less adjusted basis of your building:	$175,000	
Mortgage assumed on your old building:	– 150,000	25,000
Actual gain on exchange:		75,000
"Boot"		
Mortgage on building traded:	$150,000	
Less mortgage assumed:	145,000	
	+ 5,000	
Total gain currently taxed to you	$35,000	

Basis of New Property:

Remaining undepreciated basis of old property	$175,000
Add: Boot received (net reduction in mortgage)	+ 5,000
Tax basis of new property to be depreciated	$180,000

Three-Way Trades

It's unusual for two parties to want each other's property. Therefore the need arises for a third party. Most exchanges will involve three or more parties. For example:

A owns a six-unit building and wants B's 18-unit building. But B doesn't want A's six-unit. They need C. C wants to buy A's six-flat and will use a conventional mortgage to buy it. C will buy A's six-flat from B *after* A and B trade.

A	B	C
6-unit	18-unit	cash from mortgage loan

on the same day, A and B trade; B sells to C:

A	B	C
18-unit	6-unit	cash

result:

A	B	C
owns 18-unit	cash	owns 6-unit bought from B

The IRS watches exchanges very carefully and has challenged delayed exchanges and, so far, lost court cases in the West, the best known being the Starker Delayed Exchange. Always check with your tax attorney or accountant before attempting a delayed exchange—one that is not completed the same day.

Remember: you cannot acquire more equity in an exchange of property but must come out with what you started. In other words, you cannot trade your building with $50,000 equity for a building with $100,000 equity and realize $50,000 more equity than you started with. Your basis in the new property must remain the same.

Back to "A", "B" and "C". The original impetus to trade, buy, and sell could come from any one of them. "C" might have wanted to buy "A"'s 6-flat and "A" said "first find me a larger building to trade. I want to defer capital gains taxes." "B" may have wanted to sell the 18-flat but "C" wanted something smaller, so "B" could say "find me a smaller building to trade and then I'll sell it to you." As long as each comes out with what each wants, a trade can satisfy everyone: give "A" a tax-free exchange, "B" his sale on which he's willing to pay capital gains, and "C" the building he wants.

Exchanging will take more time and is more involved, but the rewards of having a tax-deferred exchange usually outweigh the cost in time and effort. Often the parties deferring taxes compensate the third party by giving him slightly more favorable terms in price, interest, or down payment. Always use an attorney when you embark on exchanges, and make sure your attorney has had extensive experience with the process.

TRADING YOUR HOME

Strictly speaking, a trade of homes is considered to be a sale and then a purchase. If you make an even exchange, or pay additional cash, there is no tax due on the sale of your home at that time. If you receive cash in addition to the new house, you must pay a capital gains tax on the gain, subject to the new rules, as follows:

1. You cannot sell more than one home within 18-24 months and defer taxes on any gain unless you moved to a new job location,

and your moving expenses came under I.R.S. qualifications. In that case, you may defer tax on the second sale also. As long as you keep buying homes of equal or greater value than the one you sell, you can continue to defer taxes on the gain.

2. If you are 55 years or older you may deduct $125,000 from the profit on the sale of your home, if you don't want to defer the tax, or don't buy another home within the time limit. This deduction is allowed only once in a person's lifetime. It was increased in 1981 from $100,000 to $125,000, and could be increased again—or erased—depending on future legislation.

3. A special Form 2119, Sale or Exchange of Principal Residence must be filed with the taxpayer's US income tax return in the year of sale of each residence. Special instructions apply if a new home has not yet been purchased within 24 months of the sale.

You may decide to sell your property because refinancing the equity, or trading, are not feasible. If so, consider a contract sale of the property as described in chapter 6. You can then defer capital gains taxes over the length of the contract, paying the tax only on the principal payments received each year. The interest payments will be taxed as personal income—but you can buy more real estate and shelter that income as well.

12
CONDOMINIUMS
To Go Condo—
Or Not To Go Condo

12
CONDOMINIUMS
To Go Condo—
Or Not To Go Condo

Over the past years the supply of housing has not kept pace with the demand. The resulting shortage of individual houses has caused, in turn, a short-changing of the American Dream—owning your own home. Condominiums rushed in to fill the gap, either with new constrution or conversion of rental apartment buildings. But customers didn't rush to buy them right away back in 1974. Perhaps they felt the so-called condominium was still an apartment. At any rate, they kept looking for the single-family home.

As they looked, prices went up, taxes went up, maintenance costs went up, but their salaries didn't go up quite enough. First-time buyers, in particular, were being priced out of the market. They were paying rent, that was also going up, and had nothing to show for it. Gradually, they decided that if they were ever going to own anything—even the single-family American Dream—they had to start somewhere. And that somewhere, of course, became the condominium.

Most condominium building and conversions took place in major cities and became a force for stability and growth. Not everyone is pleased with the changes wrought by condominiums, but they obviously have fulfilled a need and will continue to do so. They not only allow first-time home-buyers into the housing market, but are the answer for many "last-time" home buyers. Couples whose children have grown, and who want to limit the amount of time and care they spend on home-ownership, have also flocked to condominiums, both in cities and suburbs.

Naturally, as the demand for condominiums grew, so did the interest of investors and developers. The condominium field became a lucrative one—but one that still presents dangers to those who don't look close enough before they leap. Caution is always recommended before you invest, and the bigger the project and greater the opportunity—the bigger the opportunity to fall flat on your wallet. So take your time and:

- Seek professional help. Use a knowledgeable lawyer, real estate agent, and accountant to advise you on the legal and tax ramifications *before* you embark on condo-conversion.
- Do a feasibility study on the property to determine its potential as a condo project.
- Create a package of the property and yourself (or group) to present to a banker for financing.
- Have a marketing plan.

A WARNING TO THE SELLER

Usually when a building is sold for a condominium conversion, the seller will be paid in full. That is, if he has a mortgage presently on the property, he will receive the full purchase price and pay off that mortgage. But sometimes the mortgage is kept intact, and the seller receives only the down payment until some or all of the units are sold and ready for closing. The converter-developer prefers this arrangement in order to avoid the high interest rates charged with interim financing.

If you become the latter seller, who must wait for his money until the conversion process is completed, you need to know the risks involved and the steps to take to protect yourself. First of all, don't be in a hurry to sell to a converter. It's possible to make more money on the sale of the building to someone not interested in condominium conversion but who wants to purchase the property as a long term investment. If you are considering an offer from a developer, be sure to investigate his track record. If he has had little or no success, or experience, then you should receive a substantial earnest money deposit held by your attorney.

You need a large down payment to protect yourself should the project fold. By then you may have lost your tenants. Furthermore, the converter might claim bankruptcy at which point you would be forced to, in effect, stand in line for the money owed you. You should also be contractually protected against allowing the developer to place any liens against the property, and should receive personal guarantees from the developer as well.

In other words, if you sell your building to a converter, make sure it's really worth your while financially and contractually.

ENTERING THE CONDOMINIUM FIELD

You can invest in the condominium field three ways:

1. As a builder with new construction.

2. By purchasing a rental building to convert into condominiums.

3. By converting your own apartment building into condominiums.

This chapter will deal with numbers two and three.

Your decision will largely be based on the tax ramifications: capital gain versus ordinary income. Your lawyer and accountant can advise you on your particular situation. But one of your main concerns will be how the I.R.S. views your transactions.

The owner of a building often considers conversion to condominiums when the depreciation (tax shelter advantage) is just about used up, or no longer possible. As owner, you want to receive the highest net return possible, and try to keep your capital gains status. Chances are that if you wish to convert your building to condos the I.R.S. will consider you a dealer, thus losing any capital gains tax on the sales profit. It is more than likely that you will be taxed on all profit under ordinary income tax brackets which can go as high as 50% taxable on all profit. Many owner/converters are trying to avoid the latter of the two (dealer status).

The buyer of the property, who converts the building, will find his gain taxed as ordinary income. Therefore, he, especially, must determine what that means to his tax situation. If you will be in the 50 percent tax bracket, for instance, at the time your gain is taxed, the project may not be worth your effort. The same is true if you, as owner, discover that you will be taxed on ordinary income. Only your own advisors can give you the answers for your specific situation.

Many major condominium converters don't pay taxes on the profit for several reasons. One is that they might be a corporation and thus fall into lower tax brackets. The other major reason is that they have established a goal and in most cases own many large buildings which are being depreciated. So if they should convert one property, they will make sure that the tax write offs on the whole are greater or substantial enough to off-set any possible profit as ordinary income from a conversion. Usually a minimum tax is required.

Profits are available, risk is great and knowledge is needed especially during high interest times.

THE FEASIBILITY STUDY

Your feasibility study is meant to help you decide whether a particular building will make you more money if you, as owner, sold it outright, or converted it into a condo project; or if you, as purchaser, would gain from buying and converting a rental building to a condominium building.

First, look at the general area:

• Is the building in a good location?

• Have other condominiums sold in the area?

• Is rehabilitation going on in the area?

• Are you going to have competition selling your condos?

• Are people in the area capable of becoming home-owners?

• What is the mix of the area as to population and other types of buildings?

• Is shopping nearby or convenient?

• What is the zoning situation?

Secondly, look at the building itself:

- Is the construction above average?
- Is it architecturally appealing?
- What amenities are available? How do they compare with those offered by other condos in the general area?
- Will many improvements be necessary? Costly?
- How long will conversion take?
- What are the problem areas?
- What are the sizes and numbers of apartments?
- How long do the current leases have to run?
- Can the tenants afford to buy their apartments?

Thirdly, look at the financial aspects:

- Is financing available?
- What will be the cost of rehabilitation?
- What will be the cost of conversion?
- What are the current rents (which will probably determine the top amount you can ask for the apartments once converted and still get the tenants to buy)?
- How long will you need the financing? The transition period?
- What is the state of the economy in general (which will affect the sale of your condos)?
- Will the building make you more money as a condo project, or, as an outright sale of income property?

Naturally, the more positive features revealed by your feasibility study, the better the chance the property has to be a successful condominium project.

COST PROJECTIONS

It won't be known exactly how much money will be needed in order to convert, prior to meeting with the banker. At best you should be able to show some realistic projections of the costs.

You will be relying heavily on professionals in the business to supply you with the needed information and costs of the conversion. You should be able to obtain estimates or exact costs on some of the following items:

1. Prepayment penalties in the mortgage documents for early payment of the building mortgage. They may be reduced or waived because the banks usually welcome early payment of the mortgage balance to eliminate an older lower interest rate.

2. Points—The bank will be able to name an amount when you discuss interim financing.

3. Attorney's fees can usually be determined or at least a rough estimate can be made by the attorney especially if the attorney has done other conversions. Usually the attorney can give an estimate of the following costs: closing costs; title charges; revenue stamps; recording fees; drafting of all legal papers necessary; zoning approval; escrow fees; contracts; credit checks on purchasers.

4. Surveys showing the building size as well as all common elements, other improvements such as garages, pools, etc., and individual units. All costs relating to the above are given by the surveyor's quote, who usually has done other buildings and will know what is involved for these costs.

5. Brokers will be charging a commission that is negotiable between the two of you. The commission is usually paid at the closing of the sale. Some real estate agencies or agents may charge or split the costs of:

6. Advertising. A budget should be set if these costs are to be shared and if the real estate agent is responsible for the advertising costs. A minimum budget should be set on your property to insure proper marketing, especially during hard selling times. Signs and printing costs will have to be budgeted and estimated.

7. Model units. Establishing a model unit or units will help in the conversion sales and might have to be re-modeled—painted, varnished, carpeted, re-fixtured, new flooring, cabinets,

counter tops, indoor/outdoor carpeting, furnished, telephone, electric and gas bills, or new appliances. These costs will vary but need consideration.

8. Engineering reports. An expert engineering company specializing in condominium conversions must be obtained. The cost of the report will be available. The results of the report will need other estimates. An engineering report will tell you and any possible purchasers (in some states) everything that might need repair or replacement within the building from top to bottom (roof to heating). It also might discuss the costs of those repairs and replacements needed.

9. Improvements. Usually cosmetic: Grass; landscaping; paint; awnings; tuckpointing; etc.

10. Rehabilitation costs. They can be obtained once you determine the market price of the unit as well as the impact of the price. In other words, could you sell the units if you stripped them entirely and reworked the floor plans to sell at a much greater price and increase the demand. These costs are usually the hardest to figure because of labor and materials needed to obtain your goal of rehabilitation as per your blue prints.

11. Operating expenses. Mortgage payments, taxes, insurance, electric, heating/cooling, scavenger, water. Remember during the conversion period, the expenses must still be paid. Some or most of these costs might increase for various reasons during the conversion—for instance more electric used because of increased work on the building.

12. Inspections. Either local or state inspections might be required to allow for enforcement to meet certain codes for conversion, (Fire protection might require sprinkler systems for any condominium buildings after a certain date. Cost will vary—so check your state as well as local municipality laws for condominiums.)

13. Miscellaneous. We'll leave this one blank and hope you won't overlook an expense or cost to convert.

Make a checklist to determine if the property has enough good points to warrant condominium sales.

Address: _____

Age: _____

Construction: *Engineers report will be more specific.*

Mix. of Units: Studio   1 Bedroom   2 Bedrooms   3 Bedrooms

        # _____   _____   _____   _____

Closets per Unit:_____

Storage Space: _____   Where located:_____

Kitchen: _____   Size: Eat-in __ Cabineted __

Dining Room _____   Size:_____

Living Room: _____   Size:_____

Family Room: _____   Size:_____

Bathrooms: _____

Appliances: _____

        Stove: _____   Type of energy: _____

        Refrigerator: _____   Type of energy: _____

        Dishwasher:_____   Type of energy: _____

        Garbage disposal: ____   Type of energy: _____

        Washer: _____   Location: _____

        Dryer: _____   Location: _____

        Carpeting: _____   Where located:_____

Amenities:

Balconies: _____ Pool: _____ Sundeck: _____

Tennis: _____ Golf: _____ Club House: _____

Meeting Room: _____ Elevator: _____ Master TV: _____

Patio: _____ Fireplace: _____ Sauna: _____

Exercise Room:_____ Whirlpool:_____ Security:_____

Wet Bar: _____ Intercom: _____ Central Vacuum: _____

Parking:_____ # of spaces_____

        Carports: _____ Garages: _____

Heating: _____

Cooling: _____

Electric: _____

Plumbing: _____

Water: City: _____ Well: _____ Septic: _____ Sewer: _____

Refuse: _____

Roof: _____

- Rent of each unit
- Breakdown of leases
- Size of each unit (sq. footage)
- View of each unit
- Schools in area, shopping, industry, transportation, parks
- Monthly maintenance (what does it include)
- Estimate of taxes
- Amount of money needed to improve each unit
- Common areas
- Local municipal requirements
- Restrictions—to be imposed by developer prior to condominium association being formed

In order to insure a smooth conversion period you will need the services of a good attorney and real estate broker. Here is a list of what each might handle:

ATTORNEY:
- Laws effecting condominium conversions both local and state
- Declarations preparation
- Contract preparation
- Zoning appeals
- Trust agreements and documents
- Escrow accounts
- Closing of units sold
- Title transfers
- Recordings of papers
- Condominium association fees and future establishment of the association

- Financing legal end
- Structure of sale ownership corporation, partnership, other
- Prorations of taxes, insurance, electric, gas, water
- Meetings
- Follow up
- Check over all papers
- Organize the conversion process

BROKER:

- Do the overall analysis
- Feasibility study
- Comparable sales
- Set up lenders, financing
- Property management
- Advertise units for sale—grand opening—publicity
- Establish floor time, open house, man telephones in model unit
- Structure prices along with seller
- Printing—signs
- Qualifications of tenants residency and purchasers outside
- Meeting with appraisers, surveyor, engineer, and other agents
- Market the units
- Organize and follow up on all showings, sales and closings

LISTING AGREEMENT

When you list your building with a real estate agent, include the following items in the exclusive to avoid any misunderstandings:

- Address
- Commission

- Price
- Terms of agreement
- Financing
- Advertising budget (who pays?)
- Model units (who pays and where will they be?)
- Printing—signs
- Bonus—for quick sell-out
- Phone service
- Duties
- Length of agreement
- No automatic renewal clauses
- Clause—stating 30 day written notice by either party to release exclusive listing
- Co/op brokers—M.L.S. service
- Who pays closing costs
- Consideration for aborted project if not broker's fault
- Dated and signed

Use an attorney to draft the exclusive listing to avoid problems.

FINANCING

Remember, as with any investment, you are competing for financing. You want to prove to your financial source that you are not only a good financial risk, but that you are in control of your project. Therefore, you should prepare a package of the property and yourself (or group) before you make an appointment with a banker. (Details on preparing a package can be found in Chapter 6.) You will be asking for two types of loans: interim and permanent. And you will need both commitments from the very beginning. Banks and Savings and Loans will require an appraisal of the property for both types of financing. Make sure that they consider the appraisal as a condo and not an apartment sale. Also check the rules and regulations attached to any government loans that might be available for your project.

Interim Financing

Interim financing is similar to a construction loan. The interim loan is usually issued at 2 to 3 percent above the prime rate, and payments can be deferred until the note is due: usually six months to a year. At that time both principal and interest are due. If a problem arises, you can often renew or extend the note by paying just the interest due at due-date.

The interim loan should cover the mortgage—first or second mortgage which must be paid off prior to conversion—any prepayment penalties, remodeling and restoration costs, taxes, surveys, attorney's fees, interest, and any other expenses involved with the conversion. You can see how important it is to avoid under-budgeting, and to calculate the true expenses needed to be covered. Try not to over-budget because interim financing is expensive and will affect your profit, depending on the length of the loan and the prime rate of interest. *Keep the financing as simple as possible.*

Permanent Financing

The lender who is considering permanent financing on the individual units, will not commit their money until at least 51 percent of the units have contracts. Therefore, you will usually be able to pay off your interim loan after 51 percent of the property has been sold. It can then be considered a condominium building and closing can be set on the units. Normally, your interim lender will require that you have some permanent financing available before they will give you the first loan. Once you have paid off your interim loan, the sale of the balance of the units will give you your profit.

Timing is very important. Don't underestimate the amount of time needed to convert the property. Price the units properly so you can get in and out. Your permanent lender will give you a written commitment saying that a certain amount of money will be put aside for those qualified purchasers of your units. Once this commitment is bought, even if market conditions change (interest rates go up), you will be locked in at the agreed-upon rate for the agreed-upon term. You usually will have to pay for the end-loan commitments, or "buy" the money.

CLOSING AND RECORDING

After 51 percent of the units are sold, you can expect to have a closing. The remaining units will have closings shortly after they're sold. You and your attorney then have to consider the proper time to record the master deed. Be careful not to record near the end of the fiscal year or the I.R.S. will compute taxes on the project based on the valuation for resale as a condominium instead of on the old apartment building basis.

The master deed is usually filed with architectural plans and a survey. As soon as the deed is recorded, the real estate taxing authorities will assess the project based on the value placed on its sale as a condominium, instead of a rental building. Once the condo is recorded and declared, the owner must pay the monthly maintenance and condo charges for each unsold unit.

MARKETING

You have your broker, your attorney, and your building, and are ready to begin the marketing of your condominium units. Don't leave it to chance—or to casual planning. When your broker begins the residency program he must have all the sales information: costs, prices, improvements, maintenance, and the advantages of owning. In order to successfully market your units, you must consider the following factors:

- Pricing of the units
- Costs for prospective purchasers
- Timing of your presentation
- Selling to tenants
- Selling to outsiders

Pricing of the Units

Your first priority is the pricing of the individual units. Find out what comparable condos in your area have sold for, and when. Structure the purchase price so that your buyers will ultimately pay less, *after tax savings,* than they were paying for rent. Keep in mind the buyers' advantages of appreciation and equity. Some guidelines—price will be affected by location, amenities, and other feasibility factors pertaining to the property. Some guidelines are:

- Condominiums are usually priced about 20 to 35 percent below single family houses with similar square footage and amenities, depending on the area.

- Prices are usually established between 100 to 150 times the monthly rental for the unit.

Costs for Prospective Purchasers

Since financing is already arranged, you can usually provide purchasers with information about principal and interest. You must also include taxes, insurance, and monthly maintenance charges.

Timing of Your Presentation

It's important to begin your residency program well in advance (two to three months) of lease expirations in order to avoid possible loss of revenue caused by vacancies. A check of the leases will help you determine when more tenants are likely to move—usually at the end of their lease. You must also consider the amount of time you are going to grant tenants in deciding whether or not they will buy a unit.

In order to avoid rumors, advise each tenant of the conversion as soon as possible. Rumors spread quickly and usually start the project off on the wrong foot. Most states and cities require a time limit for this notification to the tenants.

Selling to Tenants

Your best buyer is the tenant—and every effort should be made to get them to invest and thereby cut your outside selling expenses. Each resident should be contacted personally, with a private meeting set up in their unit. You can tell them what will be done to their unit to improve it, and they can visualize the changes. They will also be more at ease in familiar surroundings. Your broker must be able to answer all questions, including:

- The tenant "discount" if they purchase within a certain period of time.

- A tenant "early bird" discount, if purchased sooner.

- Is unit for sale as is, or with new appliances, carpeting, painting, etc?

- Will you offer a buy-back agreement? This option usually increases the closing ratio of tenants by building confidence and good will.

After you have made the original presentation, you are ready to show the tenants the highly visible improvements, such as landscaping, carpeting of common areas, painting of halls, planting of flowers and shrubs, etc. These improvements can be emphasized in a series of cocktail parties and dinners arranged for the tenants for the purpose of encouraging them to purchase a unit. Hold the cocktail parties in the model unit. Many tenants hold off visiting the model unit for fear another tenant will see them and ask questions they aren't ready to answer. Once they've been in the model unit, it's also easier for tenants to stop back in later to ask more questions.

Consider running an ad to invite outside people, who have viewed the model unit, to the cocktail party, too. Their presence will increase the pressure on tenants to make a decision, and can increase the number of tenant sales. You will also have a chance to begin your outside marketing strategy.

Tenants with long-term leases (which cannot be broken in order to get them to move), and who are unsure of purchasing, can be offered a rental credit towards their purchase of a unit. You can also sell a long-term leased unit to an investor, and sweeten the pot by offering to pay assessments for a year, or closing costs.

Expect more tenants to buy a unit in a building that is in good condition and has higher rents. (Remember: the more positive factors on the feasibility study, the better chance of a successful conversion.) People in low-rent and lower income brackets usually can't afford additional expense. Those with higher incomes are more likely to be able to come up with the funds needed for a purchase.

On the average, one-third of the tenants will purchase a unit; however, even in high rental buildings, the percentage rarely exceeds

35 percent. Nevertheless, there have been buildings in which no tenants purchased a unit, but the project was still successful. Obviously, the more tenants you sell, and the faster you do it, the faster you will reach the 51 percent of sales you need in order to exchange your interim financing for permanent.

Selling to Outsiders

Once you have determined which tenants will become purchasers, you can begin your sales to the public. By this time most improvements should be completed and model units available for viewing. Start out with a grand opening, offering the public refreshments and any other incentives you can include at the time. Make sure you have enough people to show the units to and discuss the good features of the property. After the party, follow up on those first-time viewers to get their reactions. These will help you tailor the rest of your advertising and marketing campaign.

Continue with ads in local papers, open houses, and special offers to the public for a limited time. Stick to your budget because a sell-out period is almost impossible to predict. Your program should be set up so that you can get in and out, with few problems within one year. You have a good shot at it if you:

- Plan your marketing program well from the beginning.

- Make sure your professional team is organized and prepared.

- Are fair—don't gouge—give the buyers what they pay for.

- Have some sort of financing available for the purchaser.

GENERAL INFORMATION

A declaration is a group of legal papers which will contain a description of the land and the units in the building. It will set forth the percentage interest per unit and will contain the covenants and restrictions as to the use and occupancy of the unit and common areas. It will include other pertinent information required by the state condominium laws and its recording. Through a declaration, the property will be submitted to the condominium act.

By-laws provide for the election of a board of directors to

manage and operate the property. They also give authority to call meetings, provide maintenance and care for all common areas and set up the collection of assessments and other provisions that are consistent with the law. They usually cover whether or not professional management is needed.

In Illinois, the condominium association must file a corporate report and pay corporate tax. Check your local and state regulations regarding condominiums.*

The purchaser of a condo acquires the fee simple title to the air space in their unit with an undivided interest in the common elements, based upon a percentage of the building (usually based on square footage, or sales price). Common elements are everything except the unit and the air space of the unit. All the unit owners own land as tenants in common, along with other common elements: roof, laundry room, pool, etc. A buyer will receive the deed to the property after the declaration is recorded, usually at closing. For his own protection, 51 percent is the requirement for the lender's closing.

Leases must be honored by the owner or new owner.

Owner Insurance: Make sure you have fire and extended coverage on all common elements. Usually only one policy will insure the entire building. Make sure that there is total liability insurance on the building, for if someone is injured, he could bring action against the entire building if injured within a common element. The declaration will note the type of insurance. Ask your attorney to include in the declaration a notice for the individual unit owners to obtain fire and extended coverage. In case a fire should start within the unit itself, the individual must have this coverage to protect everyone else.

It is important to note that there are other types of condominium conversions being done today. Many commercial condominiums and office condominiums have been developed over the past couple of years. The result is a continued rise in the overall development of condominiums. Don't limit yourself to apartment buildings. Look for the possibility of converting other real estate, such as: strip shopping centers; professional office complexes; etc.

Remember that what you do before you go condo is as important as what you do afterwards. The legal and tax provisions that govern conversions are regularly changing and expanding. Be sure you use an attorney and an accountant who keep abreast of such changes. Follow our suggested procedures and increase your opportunities for success.

*In Illinois, the percentage of ownership of common areas is based upon the original sales price. Florida uses square footage. Check your area to see how common elements are structured.

13
SELLING TIPS
All's Well That Sells Well

13
SELLING TIPS
All's Well That Sells Well

At some point you may decide to sell your property. At least we hope you can do it as part of your own decision and not because you've become a must-seller. In either event, you have two choices—sell it with a licensed real estate agent, or sell it by yourself.

CHOOSING AN AGENT

If you decide to use a real estate agent, you must understand what the agent should do for you, and therefore how to pick the best agent to handle your listing. You don't only choose an agent, but an office, or realty company. So first of all try to choose an agent you know, and one who will, if possible, give you the best price on a commission. But you also have to consider which office has the most to offer in services, such as:

- Are they are member of a MLS (Multiple Listing Service) which gives your listing greater exposure?

- Do they offer a computerized service?

- Are they members of a national service that possibly deals with transferees?

- Do they have other listings in your area, or do they have clients who might be interested in your area?

- Can they appraise your home as well as give you comparables on other, similar properties that have sold in your area?

- How large a staff do they have to market the property?

- Will their staff preview the property before the advertising appears in the paper?

- Are they going to have an open-house, or have special pamphlets made to be distributed to interested parties?

- Will they provide mail-out service to other real estate offices?

- Do they specialize in commercial, condominium, business, residential, industrial, vacant land, farm, etc. properties, or will they be learning at your expense?

- How realistic are they about the selling period?

- How much do they know about creative financing, investment analysis, buyer qualification, marketing strategies, etc.?

- Will the listing agent appear at all showings in order to make sure that the other agent covers key points that may be overlooked?

In other words, the more a real estate office knows about your type of property, as well as about market conditions, the better equipped they are to sell your property at a good price and in a fair amount of time. It's also better to work with an agent with whom you feel secure, who also handles real estate as a full-time job. This type of agent is better for you than a relative or friend who dabbles in real estate part-time. You might be able to get the friend or relative a referral fee of 10 per cent or 20 percent of the listing, if you feel some obligation to them.

Duties of the Agent

An agent's duties can vary from listing to listing, depending on what type you have arranged between you. Usually it's the agent's responsibility to promote and market the property, find a qualified buyer, negotiate the transaction, and aid in the closing. Many times the above services are extremely involved and much more takes place behind the scenes than the buyer or seller knows about. A good agent uses all efforts to keep the transaction going forward, recognizing the timing needs of all parties, working with attorneys, accountants, relatives and anyone else who may become involved. In short, a good real estate office and agent are invaluable in bringing the sale of your property to a fruitful end.

TYPES OF LISTINGS

There are five types of listings: exclusive; owner-agency; net;

open; and flat-fee/exclusive.

Exclusive Listing

With an exclusive listing, you are letting one real estate agent and office handle the sale of your property for a period of time anywhere from 30 days to one year, depending on the type of property and the difficulties involved. Most homes and marketable apartments and commercial properties are listed for an average of 90 to 120 days, allowing the agent enough time to institute marketing strategies and have them take effect.

The office might work with a MLS (Multiple Listing Service) which increases the exposure of your property. The office that has the listing agrees to cooperate on the sale with another member of the MLS and will split the commission upon the sale of your property should another office find a buyer. Note that with an exclusive listing, the agent handles all forms of marketing the property—you do not have the right to sell it yourself. Unless you are a real estate expert, or wish to become involved, an exclusive listing is best for you, because the agent takes on the tasks of qualifying the buyers, placing ads, putting up signs, spreading the word that the property is "for sale," educating the buyer on financing methods, finding possible sources of mortgage money, holding the transaction together, and following up on closing details.

Owner-Agency

In this type of listing, the owner retains the right to sell the property, and if he does so, doesn't pay a commission to the real estate agent. Listings of this type are more common with business properties, and agents take them only if they feel they can sell the property quickly, or can beat out a rival agent for the listing. They also hope the owner will eventually turn the property into an exclusive listing. The agent's office will usually do very little advertising of this type of listing because they don't want to invest much advertising money when they can't be guaranteed a commission. The seller's exposure is thereby limited, and the length of time to sell the property is increased.

Net Listing

Net listings are outlawed in some states and considered undesirable in other states. In this type of listing, the agent guarantees that the owner will receive a net price on the sale of the property. The agent then must list the property at a higher price in order to make a profit. Neither party is happy with this type of listing because the seller always feels he might have received more money (particularly if the selling price is considerably above the net price the seller receives); the agent stands to make very little in those cases where the selling price is close to the net price. If a real estate agent does offer this type of listing, then you should seek the advice of an appraiser in order to learn the true value of your property, and also have your lawyer review all documents before you sign.

Open Listing

With the open listing, the owner retains the right to sell the property himself, while at the same time offering the open listing to any number of real estate agents, but not on an exclusive basis. Therefore the owner pays a commission only to the real estate agent who sells the property. Should the owner sell it himself, no commisison is due any other agent. Normally, nothing has to be signed in order to establish an open listing. The real estate industry frowns upon this type of listing because an agent can put in a lot of time and effort and end up with nothing, and sometimes a conflict of interest arises when an agent and the owner each claim the buyer.

Flat-Fee Exclusives

In this type of listing, the agency performs its services for a flat fee, and the owner shows his own property. The agency will set the appointment, qualify the buyer, draft the contract and negotiate the transaction. The owner, however, does not have the right to sell the property himself during the period of the listing contract. In some cases, if the property is not sold, the owner still owes the flat-fee agreed upon.

HOW COMMISSIONS WORK

It's important to remember that commissions are negotiable. It's unlawful for real estate agents in a community to create fixed-price commissions. They can start at 0 percent and go to infinity. However most areas have commissions that range within a couple of percentage points.

You can negotiate a commission either at the time you sign a listing agreement or when a contract is presented. Before signing any listing agreement, you should have interviewed four or five agents. Some may have told you that you have a marketable property and perhaps suggested that you lower your asking price in light of market conditions or sales of similar properties. Let's say that they all seem eager to get your listing. You, then, choose the agent you think would do the best job and say, "I'd like to use you, but your commission is too high. I want to pay (name a figure). If you can reduce your commission, fine. If you can't, there are four other agencies interested in my building." The agent knows you've interviewed the others and one of them may go along. But if the agent refuses, you might say, "I reduced my price to your suggested amount, and you say I have a marketable property. If you're right, it should sell quickly. So I'll pay you your full commission if you sell the property in 30 days. You'll have earned it. But if you haven't brought me a reasonable offer within 30 days, then you reduce your commission by 1 percent, and again, if no offer within 60 days, you drop another percent."

If you do have a marketable property, chances are the agent will go along with you. If not, you can wait until the contract comes in. Assuming it's for less than your asking price, as it usually is, then you can tell your agent, "You're asking me to accept this lower amount. If you'll cut your commission, I'll sign." If the listing period is about to run out, and you've indicated that you are thinking of changing agents, the agent may agree. When an agent is that close to a sale, or losing a listing, he often will cooperate.

The commission agreed upon in the listing can be split in the following ways:

Real Estate Agent A lists a property for sale which was sold by

Agent B, in another office, for $300,000. If the commission was 6 percent of the gross sales price, then $18,000 would be due, and the two offices would split that 50/50, each receiving $9,000. The two agents would then split the $9,000 with their offices, depending on the agreement within an office. If 50/50, then the agent would receive $4,500 and the office keeps $4,500. If the agreement is 60/40, then the agent receives $5,400 and the office $3,600.

If two agents are in the same office, and one has listed the property, and one has sold it, the office receives the $18,000, but the agents split the $9,000 agent-share according to the rules of that office. Again, one can receive 60 percent and the other 40 percent. In either case, the office keeps $9,000 because they were the listing and selling office. The agents split because one was the listing agent and the other the selling agent.

If the sales person who lists the property is also the one who sells it, then the full $18,000 again stays in the office and is divided according to the agreement between broker and salesperson. If it's 50/50 then the sales person receives $9,000.

If a broker has several good agents in the office, then they all can do very well.

FOR SALE BY OWNER (FSBO)

If you have decided to go it alone and market your property yourself, the following tips can help you arrive at a reasonable selling price and handle the sale and negotiations:

- Find out what properties are selling for in your area. If possible, get comparables of the area, and an appraisal. You can find an appraiser through your bank or savings and loan; a local real estate office; or in your phone book under an M.A.I. listing (Member of Appraisal Institute). Costs of appraisals can vary.

- Outline your objective: the amount of money you can expect to net. Figure your equity first in order to determine the amount of profit available to you.

- Try to sell your property for a realistic price; don't let your ego dictate what you'll get or be willing to accept. The market will decide that.

- Determine whether you fall into a "must-sell" category, and therefore how much cash you'll need for whatever purpose you have in mind.
- Have your accountant or tax advisor help you determine what the tax consequences will be on the sale; try to plan ahead so you can avoid an unnecessary tax burden. Do you need cash now, or can you take less of a down payment and possibly make more by selling on contract. (See example in taxes and depreciation chapter.)
- Be aware of the special tax situation when selling your residence. (See more details in the chapter on taxes and depreciation.) You can defer capital gains on a residence by buying another within 24 months—it must be for $1.00 more than the home you sold. Keep all receipts of any improvements you have made in order to reduce the amount of profit on the sale.

You cannot sell more than one home within 24 months and defer taxes on any gain unless you moved to a new job location, and your moving expenses came under I.R.S. qualifications. In that case, you may defer tax on the second sale also. As long as you keep buying homes of equal or greater value than the one you sell, you can continue to defer taxes on the gain.

If you are 55 years or older you may deduct $125,000 from the profit on the sale of your home. You don't have to re-invest in another home. Note that other provisions must be met as outlined in taxes and depreciation chapter. This deduction is allowed only once in a person's lifetime.

Timing is important. Anyone selling in areas that are hit by severe winter weather is more likely to be a must-seller, and will find a smaller buyer market because of holidays, reluctance to move during bad weather, to take children out of school, etc.

Have your lawyer check over your mortgage documents to determine if your mortgage is assumable, or has a call-in clause (if you sell on contract, your mortgage might be due and payable in full upon the sale, also called due-on-sale).

- Check with your bank about the mortgage and whether it's assumable. Ask if they will let you refinance, or if they have special financing at a lower rate should you send them a buyer who wishes to get a mortgage through them. Remember, you wish to deal with the bank or savings and loan that wants to work with you, and it's important to use those contacts that are available to you.

- Make up information sheets that contain the following information: Style and age of property; lot size, taxes, garage, special features such as pool, sprinkler for lawn, fireplace, built-in appliances, thermo-pane windows, etc. For income property include the number of units, condition of building, any special or new features such as remodeled units, new(er) boiler, roof, water-heater, electrical work; whether it's fully occupied, has off-street parking, etc.

    Try to have receipts available for the current year's bills. You can write the utility company, giving your account number and they'll provide photo-copies. You'll need these to verify expenses prior to closing.

- Also make up a financial sheet with the following information: break-down of the rental from each unit; security deposits; decorating deposits; key deposits; lease start and expiration dates; and whether the tenants have options for renewal; escalation clauses on the options; whether they are net, net net, or net net net leases. Do they have provisions for added funds such as percentage leases in which the owner gets a percentage of the tenant's profit over an agreed-upon base? Do all the calculations for at least a full year and have these figures available. The following is an example of a financial sheet that should be available to buyers:

Gross income (including washers and dryers) $ _____

> Expenses:
> Taxes $ _____
> Insurance $ _____
> Fuel (Heat—gas, oil, electric) $ _____
> Electric $ _____
> Water $ _____
> Garbage pick-up $ _____
> Janitor $ _____
> Miscellaneous $ _____
> Total expenses $ _____
> Net income $ _____

- Determine general market conditions and potential buyers for your property so you can gear your advertising properly. You can spotlight any of the following: owner financing; assumable mortgage; below-market-rate available; V.A. or F.H.A.; low down payment; priced to sell; owner transferred; estate sale, etc.

- Try to determine what it is about your property that will appeal to a buyer. Draft several forms of ads, focusing on the main points.

- Don't put all the information in the ad or make it too large. Say just enough to attract calls, but not so much that buyers decide they don't want your property without ever seeing it. Make sure the information flows naturally and isn't confusing. Following are two examples:

Lake Shore Area

Deluxe three bedroom ranch w/2 car detached garage, many extras, possible owner financing 9% interest 25% down. By owner, call 222-1212 after 6 p.m.

City location—10 unit building

All brick, assumable mortgage at 7%, owner anxious. Will consider offer priced at 8 x gross, new electric, tenant heat, much more; contact owner 222-1212.

- Qualify all buyers. If you aren't using an agent who weeds out the "lookers," you'll have to do the qualifying yourself, preferably over the phone to save time. Try to find out what price range the buyer is considering; the amount he has available for a down payment, and what kind of financing he requires. Does he have sufficient income to qualify for a bank loan; does he have to sell his own property first; and does he need some or all seller financing. If you're willing to handle some or all of the financing, you especially need a buyer whose income and/or assets can assure you that the monthly payments will be made on time.

- Make sure that whoever answers your phone can give enough information to encourage the qualified buyer to come out and see your property. You can't sell the property over the phone, and buyers try to think of reasons to avoid a trip to see your property, so you need someone who can turn the call into a visit.

- Be prepared for some buyers who knock at your door at various hours, especially if you're selling your residence and have a sign on the front lawn. Also be prepared for many real estate agents calling or knocking at your door. Competition is keen and what better way to get a listing from someone who wants to sell than from a "for sale by owner." Many will say they have buyers for your property. If that is the case, you might allow them to show the property on an open listing, and if a contract does develop you can agree on a commission for that buyer if the deal goes through.

- When you're handling the sale yourself, before you sign any agreement, especially with a buyer, use your lawyer at a very early stage. You won't have the advice of a real estate agent to tell you what is a normal transaction or one that may tie up your property and hurt you.

- Especially beware of the "contingent buyer" who must sell or close on another transaction in order to buy your property. If their property doesn't sell or close within a specified time, they won't purchase your property. While a contingent buyer can also appear with a real estate agent, the follow-up actions can be different unless the owner stays right on top of the deal, and finds out how the potential buyers are going about selling the property *they* must sell in order to buy yours. An agent would make sure that you have the normal contingent contract which means your property stays on the market and can be sold to someone else who isn't a contingent buyer. Your position becomes more secure because once the first buyer, or even the second, knows someone else wants the property, they want it even more. The trouble with contingent buyers in a tight market is that many transactions fall through, and the owner meanwhile sits tight, instead of following up on the deal.

  For instance: Suppose the Smiths want to buy your property but must sell their property first, and therefore need more time. If the Smiths are selling their property themselves, it's important for you to check on where their property is located, what price they're asking, especially in comparison with other properties in the area. Check on what they are doing to find a buyer, and what kind of buyer (cash, V.A., F.H.A., etc.), and what kind of advertising they use. Furthermore, try to find out how flexible they are about getting their price and terms, and how long their property has been for sale. The more you know about how they plan to sell *their* property, the better position you'll be in to know whether it's likely that they'll be able to follow through on their transaction with you.

- Regardless of how fast or slow you think the contingent buyer will handle the sale of his property, *never allow a clause that forbids you from continuing to market your property, or that allows them an unreasonable period of time to meet any other bid you might get from a non-contingent buyer.* A normal contingency clause gives the buyer 30 to 60 days to firm up (drop their contingency) and move forward with the purchase.

The clause also states that you may continue to market your property, but if you find another buyer (non-contingent), the first contingent-buyer has an agreed-upon time (24, 36, 48 hours) in which to firm up their offer, and drop all contingencies, or withdraw from their attempted purchase.

- The problem with giving a contingent buyer a longer period than 60 days, is that you are tempted to believe you have a purchaser, and may stop advertising, and if the deal falls through you have lost time and have nothing to show for it.

- Make sure your lawyer reviews all papers before you sign, or insert a clause that allows your lawyer to review the papers and make changes within a period of time after the signing.

- Have closing at the end of the month.

Follow-up Tips (Once you've found a buyer)

1. Meet with your lawyer/accountant to check out the contract, smoothing out any differences, and have it signed by all parties. Make several copies.

2. Give a copy of the title policy to buyer's attorney. (It's needed to order a title search or bring down title.)

3. Give the buyers your lawyer's name, phone number, and address so they can reach him quickly if necessary.

4. Find out where the buyers are going to apply for a mortgage.

5. Follow-up any information you have on their application: keep a record of dates of phone calls and people you talked to in checking their information.

6. Get the legal description of the property from the title policy for a survey, if applicable.

7. Open an escrow account, and deposit any necessary papers, if applicable. Lawyers can establish an escrow account or act as an escrow agent.

8. Make sure your lawyer has all the information necessary about the buyer's lawyer and encourage contact between them to pre-

vent delays. Follow up with your lawyer to see if anything is needed, or if all is going smoothly. Don't *assume* all is well just because you haven't heard anything.

9. Lawyers will establish closing procedures on escrow.

10. Close transaction.

Rent with Option to Buy

If you are selling a condominium or a house, and haven't had much action, change your ad to read: "Rent with an Option to Buy."

It is much better for you to rent with an option to buy than it is to give the property to a real estate agent for six months as an exclusive listing to sell. For one thing, you can explain to the tenant that if he fulfills the terms of the lease, you will allow him one or two thousand dollars of the rent paid by him as a credit towards his down payment. And you will be receiving rent instead of making monthly payments on an empty piece of real estate. (See chapter 7 for details from buyer's point of view as well.)

Be sure the tenant has good credit and already has a sufficient amount in savings for a down payment. Otherwise, you will find it hard to get financing for him or will be unwilling to finance him yourself.

People are usually looking for rent-with-an-option-to-buy advertisements because they realize they can often get a good deal, and the arrangement gives them time to see if they like the area. Another selling option is the lease-purchase arrangement described in chapter 7.

Whether you choose a real estate agent to sell your property, or decide to do it yourself, use the selling tips as a guide and checklist. As with any product, if you present it properly, price it fairly, and simplify the buying procedure, making it easy and pleasant for the buyer to buy, you will make a sale. And then if you apply the techniques described in this book, you'll be able to make another good buy.

14
TAXES &
DEPRECIATION
Or Profits—
Now You See Them—
Now You Don't

14
TAXES &
DEPRECIATION
Or Profits—
Now You See Them—
Now You Don't

The following chapter is written in the form of questions and answers. We chose this format because we believe that these are the questions you need to ask if you're going to protect yourself and make the most amount of money from your real estate investments.

How do rich people and big corporations pay so little income tax?

The tax code is structured to encourage people to take certain risks with their investments by letting them use money that would ordinarily be taxed. These incentives are called "tax shelters".

Who advises people on these "tax shelters"?

Those who can afford it hire expensive tax lawyers and accountants. They don't get advice from the I.R.S. Usually the I.R.S. will not stand behind any mistakes their employees might make. And you will pay the penalty. So, you should use the services of an accountant. Tax laws and regulations change frequently and are complex. They are also subject to new interpretations and modifications by court decisions. Therefore, grey areas result when the I.R.S. and the individual taxpayer disagree on rules that have not been challenged or interpreted by the courts. An accountant can help you stay within the guidelines as currently understood.

Why do I need to know about depreciation and capital gains?

By knowing how to figure the results of your investment, both when you buy and when the time comes to sell, you can then be in control from start to finish. And the more you know, the better the information you can give your accountant, and the better you can judge what your accountant knows.

What is a tax shelter?

Any investment or expenditure that reduces the amount of income tax you have to pay.

Are there different kinds of tax shelters?

Yes. They fall into the following five types:

1. Any *deduction* from your *income* which reduces your income tax bracket or marginal tax. The value of a deduction then depends on your tax bracket. If, after your normal deductions, you are in the 30 percent bracket (meaning every dollar of income over a certain base is taxed 30 percent), then by deducting those dollars you save 30 percent or 30 cents for each dollar deducted. If you were in the 50 percent tax bracket, every dollar you can deduct saves you 50 percent or 50 cents for each dollar deducted. Interest, taxes and operating expenses for an apartment building are examples.

2. A credit against your income *tax* which reduces your tax dollar-for-dollar. (If you have earned an energy credit, for instance, of $250, that $250 comes directly off your bill, regardless of your tax bracket.) If you buy a car or truck for your business or to manage your properties, you may be able to reduce your taxes with a 6 percent investment credit on the cost of the vehicle.

3. A deferral of your current taxes—you take a deduction this year and show as income that amount in a later year, at which time you will pay the tax due on it. The value of the tax deferral depends on your current tax bracket and your future tax bracket, as well as the length of the deferral period and infla-

tion during that period. With deferral, the I.R.S. is giving you, in effect, an interest-free loan which will be paid back with cheaper dollars because of inflation. You may also pay fewer dollars if you are then also in a lower tax bracket because of retirement. Accelerated depreciation is an example of the use of depreciation deductions to defer taxes. When rental property is sold at a gain, the prior depreciation deductions will be "recaptured" and taxes paid for the year of sale.

4. A *postponement* of gains or income until a future event or time when your tax bracket may be less and hence the tax bite smaller. Trade or exchange of property is an example of postponing gain recognition.

5. A reduction or exclusion of *income* because of a tax incentive in our tax laws. Thus the tax, if any, is paid on only part of the income and not all of it. Sometimes all income can be excluded up to a certain point as with the sale of a personal residence. The 60% exclusion for capital gains is another example.

DEPRECIATION

How does "Depreciation" apply to real estate?

Basically, a depreciation is an accounting method that allows you to deduct the value of a building over a period of time *as if* it is losing value because of age and use, even though, in most cases, the building is actually appreciating in value. In other words, the loss of a building's value is a *paper loss*. By deducting that loss (depreciation) from the profit, you save taxes.

May I take depreciation on my home?

No. You may take depreciation (deduction for wear and tear) only on income-producing properties, such as apartment buildings, condominium units and houses that are rented. If you move out of your home and rent it, you can then take the depreciation deductions as you would the other income-producing properties.

Can anything else be depreciated besides the building?

You may also depreciate the components of the building, such as appliances, and some major improvements (explained later in the chapter).

Is land value included in the depreciation?

No. Land itself is considered to have no depreciation. You must determine the value of the land and subtract it from the total purchase price to find the final figure which is the *depreciation basis* on the property.

How do I determine land value?

Four methods can be used:

1. Appraisal. It is often possible to get a breakdown of the building and land value from the lender who had it appraised originally for financing. The price of hiring an appraisal firm varies from company to company and depends on the amount of work involved. Once the price of the property is determined through an appraisal it can be used to maintain proper insurance coverage on the building because insurance companies will not insure the land. You can then attach it to the permanent record on the property for future reference.

2. Comparables. A local real estate office can get you copies of comparable *empty* lots with similar zoning that have recently sold in the general area. You can then determine the cost per square foot and apply that cost to your property. Get comparables on at least three lots. Note that if there are only a couple of vacant lots available in the area, the price for those remaining may be higher. Location also plays a role in price. Corner lots or lots on cul-de-sacs are usually higher priced.

3 Comparables

(Your property is zoned multi-family, 4-units)

	Parcel #1	Parcel #2	Parcel #3
Lot size:	100 x 150	70 x 130	90 x 150
Sq. Ft.	15,000	9,100	13,500
Use (zoning)	M.F. 4	Commercial	M.F. 6
List price	$65,000	$62,900	$67,500
Date	1/81	3/81	6/81
Sale price	$65,000	$60,000	$65,000
Price per Sq. Ft.	$4.33	$6.59	$4.81

As you can see above, the multi-family in parcel #1 and the multi-family zoned to build six units in parcel #3 range between $4.33 and $4.81 per square foot. You could average the difference—$4.57 per square foot, and multiply it by your property, which is 75 x 135, or 10,125 square feet. The value of your land comes to $46,271.25. You paid $185,000 for your 4-unit building, less $46,000 rounded off land value, which gives you $139,000 as the depreciation basis for your building.

3. Tax bill. By checking the tax bill you can determine the assessed valuation for the land and the building.

4. "Rule of Thumb." While it would be nice to assume the land had no value, the I.R.S. usually permits 15 percent to be allocated to the land cost. On the above example, 15 percent of the purchase price of $185,000, is $27,750. Subtracting that, your depreciation basis would be $157,250.

Is the depreciation based just on age?

No. There are three ways to "lose" value on a building:

1. Physical

2. Functional

3. Economical

Physical loss means the building is getting older.

Functional loss affects the inside of the building and deals with obsolescence of design (old-fashioned radiators), plumbing fixtures, room sizes, etc.

Economical loss is effected through or by economic changes in the area, such as businesses moving away to newer malls, population shifts, school closings, etc.

What is considered the "life" of a property?

The life of your property is really an economic view based on time. Business or rental property must be depreciated over its useful life, a period of time you must examine with care so as not to have problems with the I.R.S.

How do I establish the useful life of a property?

You check comparable properties in the area; obtain a statement from the contractor or architect, or by using a general guideline.

What are the guidelines?

The maximum a building can be depreciated is usually 45 years. Under the old method, prior to 1981, new buildings were often depreciated over 40 to 45 years. Recent construction usually had its age subtracted from the 40 to 45 figure. Older properties were often depreciated over 20 to 25 years, depending on age, area, construction, and condition of the building.

If you had tried to depreciate the property over a period less than the I.R.S. guidelines, the I.R.S. would probably have challenged your timetable. Your reason might have been that a new chemical plant in the area has caused problems, or that the value of your property is dropping quickly because of all three "losses"—physical, functional, and economical. On the other hand, the I.R.S. might counter by saying that your 25-year mortgage assumes the building will be used at least 25 years.

What else should I consider in determining the building's life?

Depreciation is best viewed in relation to your long range plans, the amount of personal income tax you are currently paying, when you plan to retire, and whether your personal income then might be less (lower tax bracket). Try to depreciate the property over the *shortest* period of time allowable using a depreciation method giving you the most tax deductions against current income. (Reasons and examples later in chapter.)

Should I depreciate all my properties the same way?

No. We recommend that you invest in two types of properties: those to be held for long periods of time, and those for short periods. Depreciation methods and rates can be different for each property.

Do I have to take depreciation?

Yes. If you do not depreciate your building, when you sell or trade that building the I.R.S. will compute your *allowable* depreciation over the period of time and make you "recapture" it (claim it) anyway! And meanwhile you have lost the deductions that you would have been allowed each year you owned the property.

For example: Using the new allowable S.L. method on your 10-unit bulding with a $250,000 depreciation basis, with depreciation deductions allowable of $16,666 a year over a 15-year life ($250,000 divided by 15 years = $16,666 depreciation allowable each year), assume that you do *not* take that amount of depreciation on your annual tax returns.

You sell your property five years later, and now the I.R.S. steps in to say you should have used $83,333 worth of depreciation on the property. They will add it to your profit on the property and you will pay a capital gains tax on that $83,333 even though you *never* got or used the $83,333 tax shelter allowable you. You may, however, file amended tax returns for some of these years to claim the depreciation you should have taken.

TYPES OF DEPRECIATION PRE-1981

Are there different types of depreciation?

Yes. There were four types prior to 1981:

- Straight Line
- Component
- Accelerated 125 percent, 150 percent, 200 percent
- Sum of the years (digits)

What is the Straight Line (SL) type of depreciation?

This method is the simplest and most common. It is also the least beneficial. To figure your depreciation allowance, you take the cost of the property and divide it evenly over the expected useful life of the property. Again, minus land value.

Example: $100,000 cost basis of a building; 25 years useful life under the old method.

$100,000 divided by 25 = $4,000 yearly allowance or 4 percent depreciation per year for 25 years.

In the following examples, the net income is the amount of money left over to pay the mortgage payments. The amount of cash flow would depend on the purchase price, down payment, and type of deal, such as the interest rate and amortization schedule.

	A (6-Unit)	B (12-Unit)	C (20-Unit)
Gross income	$20,880.00	$44,500.00	$69,600.00
Expenses:	$ 5,976.00	$12,000.00	$19,920.00
Net income:	$14,904.00	$32,500.00	$49,680.00
Mortgage:	$148,500.00	$315,000.00	$391,500.00
at 9% interest			
25 years: monthly	$1,246.22	$2,643.48	$3,285.47
	x 12	x 12	x 12
Yearly payment	$14,954.64	$31,721.76	$39,425.64

Note that the above amounts are almost all for interest in early years (the payments for principal reduction are considered equity and are not deductible as an expense). For simplicity, we have assumed the mortgage payments to be entirely interest in this example.

The following examples take Building A, B, and C through the computations involved in figuring depreciation advantages as a tax shelter:

	A (6-Unit)	B (12-Unit)	C (20-Unit)
Purchase price:	$165,000.00	$350,000.00	$435,000.00
Land:	− 25,000.00	− 50,000.00	− 65,000.00
Depreciation basis:	$140,000.00	$300,000.00	$370,000.00

(25 year life of improvements for each—old method)

	A (6-Unit)	B (12-Unit)	C (20-Unit)
Yearly deduction:	$ 5,600.00	$ 12,000.00	$ 14,800.00
Net income:	14,904.00	32,500.00	49,680.00
Mortgage payments:	− 14,954.64	− 31,721.76	− 30,425.64
Cash flow:	− $ 50.64	$ 778.24	$ 19,254.36

As the examples show, A has a negative cash flow, B and C have positive cash flows.

Now you claim your depreciation under the SL method:

	A	B	C
Depreciation:	− $ 5,600.00	− $12,000.00	− $14,800.00
Loss or profit:	− 50.64	+ 778.24	+ 19,254.36
Net paper loss:	$ 5,650.64(−)	$11,221.76(−)	$ 4,454.36(+)

The method and advantages are explained as follows:

Property A: Because of the negative cash flow in property A, you *add* this loss to the depreciation allowed to find your paper loss or surplus.

In the case of the $5,650.64 paper loss, you can use that amount to offset any income you have for that year, such as wages, interest, or other profit. For example: If your personal income totaled $30,000 for the year, you would be able to deduct $5,650.64 even if you do not itemize personal deductions, leaving $24,349.36. From this amount you can still deduct your other allowable deductions such as:

- interest payments on your home mortgage

- personal exemptions (family of 4 = $1,000 deduction per person)

- medical, taxes, interest, contributions, and other deductions you are entitled

Compare the following:

	With Building Loss	With No Building Loss
Wages	30,000.00	30,000.00
Building deductions	(-) 5,650.64	.00
Income before personal deductions	24,349.36	30,000.00
Personal itemized deductions $6,500.00 less standard deduction of $3,400.00	(−) 3,100.00	(−) 3,100.00
	21,249.36	26,900.00
Exemptions for family of 4	(−) 4,000.00	(−) 4,000.00
	17,249.36	22,900.00
Joint return US tax (1982)	2,283.00	3,618.00

Note that your taxes were reduced by $1,335.00. These actual tax dollars saved change the $50.64 negative cash flow from the building into a positive cash flow of $1,284.36! If your wages and other income were considerably higher than the $30,000 example, then your tax savings would be even greater because of your higher tax bracket.

Property B: With property B you must subtract cash flow (profit) from the depreciation figure ($12,000 minus $778.24) to achieve the net paper loss of $11,221.76. If we used this amount on the example for property A, then you would deduct from your $30,000 income the paper loss of $11,221.76 and eventually end up with little or no taxable income:

$30,000.00	income
- 11,221.76	building deductions
$18,778.24	
3,100.00	personal itemized deductions of $6,500 plus standard deduction of $3,400.00
15,678.24	
4,000.00	exemptions for a family of four
11,678.24	taxable income
1,198.00	joint return US tax (1982)

Net operating loss applies to a big loss *before* personal deductions.

Note that in the above example, you were able to shelter (avoid paying taxes on) your cash flow as well as most of personal income. Instead of paying income tax, you could get money back!

Property C: Property C has a very large cash flow which now comes to you tax-free by virtue of the depreciation allowed.

You still have $4,545 paper loss to use against your personal income. Using the same income figures as before:

$30,000.00	original income (gross)
- 4,545.64	building deductions
$25,454.36	
3,100.00	personal itemized deduction (as above)
22,354.36	
- 4,000.00	exemptions for a family of four
18,354.36	taxable income

You now owe taxes on only $18,354.36 because $14,800 was "sheltered" for you by depreciation. A nice way to make a living.

Note that this depreciation is figured using the SL method which allows the least amount of benefits. The other methods often yield larger depreciation amounts. Remember also that we figured a 10 percent down payment and 9 percent interest. You could achieve a larger cash flow by putting more money down, getting a lower interest rate, or purchasing the property for a lesser amount.

What is accelerated depreciation? Pre-1981

Accelerated depreciation, also called the declining balance method, depreciates the property at a faster rate which results in higher deductions during the early years of the property's useful life. Depending on your building, you might have used the 125 percent, 150 percent, or 200 percent rates which apply only to the remaining balance of the building's original basis.

How did the rates apply to different properties?

- 125 percent was allowed on used income properties
- 150 percent was allowed on used equipment and new commercial properties
- 200 percent was allowed on new equipment and new apartment buildings (less than one year old and never occupied.)

How do you figure the amount of depreciation allowed each year?

1. First figure the amount of depreciation allowed under the SL method.

2. Multiply the SL amount by the declining balance allowed:

	A (6-Unit)	B (12-Unit)	C (20-Unit)
Basis	$140,000	$300,000	$370,000
SL/year	$5,600 or 4%	$12,000 or 4%	$14,800 or 4%
Declining	x125%x4%(=5%)	x125%x4%(=5%)	x125%x4%(=5%)
Bal. 125%	$7,000 1st yr.	$15,000 1st yr.	$18,500 1st yr.

As you can see, with the accelerated method you could claim a larger amount of depreciation in the early years: $1400 more in example A, $3,000 more in B, and $3,700 more in C. Those larger amounts shelter larger cash flows and income.

Remember that in the *next* year, depreciation is based on the balance:

	A	B	C
Cost basis	$140,000	$300,000	$370,000
Dep. taken	- 7,000	- 15,000	- 18,500
x Accelerated rate	5%	5%	5%
2nd year depreciation	$ 6,650	$ 14,250	$ 17,575

(To use the accelerated 150 percent method and 200 percent method you would again compute the SL percentage first, then multiply by 1.5 or 2.0, deducting the total each year in order to figure the depreciation on the balance.)

Note that the third year results in fewer dollars for depreciation, but they are still greater than the straight line amount:

	A	B	C
Original cost basis (excluding land)	$140,000	$300,000	$370,000
Original straight line depreciation for 25 years (100% ÷ 25 years = 4% Rate)	$ 5,600 Per Year	$ 12,000 Per Year	$ 14,800 Per Year
1st Year Balance	$140,000	$300,000	$370,000
1st Year Accelerated Depr.	$ 7,000	$ 15,000	$ 18,500
2nd Year Balance	$133,000	$285,000	$351,500
2nd Year Accelerated Depr.	$ 6,650	$ 14,250	$ 17,575
3rd Year Balance	$126,350	$270,750	$333,925
3rd Year Accelerated Depr.	$ 6,317	$ 13,537	$ 16,696
4th Year Balance	$120,033	$257,213	$317,299

Because you had the most depreciation in the early years, you can see that eventually the amount would shrink and shelter less cash flow and income. In addition, that extra amount of depreciation is subject to a tax on its "recapture."

What is a recapture tax?

The accelerated method of depreciation provides greater deductions and therefore may seem like a gift from the I.R.S., but it is really only a loan and is taxed or recaptured. In other words, they tax the amount of extra depreciation obtained beyond the straight line method at the tax rate for ordinary income, and not capital gains.

For example: If you could have earned $15,000 depreciation on the SL method, and you used the accelerated 125 percent method, you realized an $18,750 depreciation, or $3,750 more. This excess amount is taxable, when the building is sold, as ordinary income at your normal income tax rate. However, the amount realized on the SL method is subject to the capital gain exclusion of 60 percent and the remaining 40 percent is taxed at your income tax rate. (If your tax bracket is 40 percent —your capital gains would be 16 percent.) The amount of taxable income recaptured depends on how long you own the property and what type of accelerated depreciation you used.

Recapture is taxable only when you sell the property and in some cases can be avoided by trading.

What is Component Depreciation? Pre-1981

Component depreciation was an offshoot of the SL method.

Instead of depreciating the building as a whole, it was broken down into its major parts (components). These parts were assigned useful-life years and were depreciated separately. It is assumed that the basic structure would last longer than some of its replaceable components.

The component method resulted in a faster depreciation than the SL method and was not favored by the I.R.S. In fact, this method is not permitted for property purchased in 1981 and later years under President Reagan's 1981 tax law changes. It was preferred by the I.R.S. to restrict its use to new construction where the cost of the building's components were known. Nevertheless, if you get a professional appraisal that breaks down the costs of an existing building, you may be allowed to continue this method of depreciation for property purchased before 1981. There was no recapture tax levied on the component method.

An example of the method follows:

25-Year-Old 12-Unit Building, Purchase price: $350,000
Land value: 50,000
Depreciation basis: $300,000

Improvements	Life of Improvements	Cost	Rate	Allowance Per Year
Structure	20 years	$200,000	5.00%	$10,000
Roof and chimney	10 years	$ 44,000	10.00%	$ 4,400
Personal property (Stoves, refrigerator)	7 years	$ 28,000	14.29%	$ 4,000
Electrical, plumbing	7 years	$ 28,000	14.29%	$ 4,000
Totals		$300,000		$22,400

At the end of one year you could claim a depreciation of $22,400. You could claim this figure for seven years, at which time personal property, electrical and plumbing would be fully depreciated. Depreciation would continue for three more years at the remaining $14,000 per year, then $10,000 per year.

Had you used the SL method for a 20-year period of useful life, you would be allowed to deduct only $15,000 depreciation per year.

Should you sell the property, you would add up the amount of depreciation used and add it to your profit on which you pay a capital gains tax. If you trade properties, in effect, you carry over the amount of depreciation to the new property and deduct it from that property's basis which will give you a new basis of depreciation. (See chapter on trading.)

What is the Sum of the Digits Depreciation?

This fast depreciation method is only permitted for new residential buildings or new equipment prior to 1981. You add up the sum total of the years over which you plan to depreciate the property. For example, if you were depreciating a building over 25 years, you would add up the following:

$$1 + 2 + 3 + 4 + 5 + 6 + 7 + 8 + 9 + 10 + 11 + 12 + 13 + 14 +$$
$$15 + 16 + 17 + 18 + 19 + 20 + 21 + 22 + 23 + 24 + 25$$

This equals 325. Then for the first year you would be able to claim 25/325 of the property basis as depreciation. The second year you would deduct 24/325, and so on until the 25th year when you would be claiming 1/325 deduction as depreciation. When you use this method you will be depreciating the property to the end of its useful life.

The following example is for an 8-unit building at $250,000 with a 25-year life: (You divide $250,000 by 325 which is $769.23. This amount is subtracted every year.)

Year 1	$19,230.75	Year 9	$13,076.91	Year 17	$6,923.07
2	18,461.52	10	12,307.68	18	6,153.84
3	17,692.29	11	11,538.45	19	5,384.61
4	16,923.06	12	10,769.22	20	4,615.38
5	16,153.83	13	9,999.99	21	3,846.15
6	15,384.60	14	9,230.76	22	3,076.92
7	14,615.37	15	8,461.53	23	2,307.69
8	13,846.14	16	7,692.30	24	1,538.46
				25	769.23

Again you can see that most of the depreciation comes in the early years.

To sum up, depreciation has the following aspects to consider:

1. What is being depreciated   Personal property, real estate, or improvements.

2. Age at purchase   New or used.

3. Cost of property   Purchase cost, inherited basis or traded basis.

4. Deduct for residual value   Do not depreciate land value or equipment salvage value.

5. Remaining life of property   Depends on current age plus economic and other factors

6. Method of depreciation   Straight life, declining balance, component or other variations.

7. What are your ultimate goals from depreciation   Consider: your current tax bracket, future tax brackets, period of time until retirement, length of time expected to hold property, other income sources.

Can I defer capital gains tax by re-investing?

No. Investment property rules differ from those that apply to your home (place of residence). You cannot defer capital gains tax unless you exchange your real estate property or sell it on contract. When you sell your home you can defer any capital gains tax by investing in another home within 24 months before or after the sale. You must pay at least $1.00 more for your new home in order to defer all your capital gains. (Taxpayers 55 years and older are allowed one time exclusion of $125,000 after July 20, 1981.)

Must I re-invest all the profit I make on the sale of my own home?

No. You can use leverage (borrowed money, loans) and keep

most of the profit when you sell one home and move to a more expensive one. The new house must simply *cost* more—but you need not put more money down, or any money down, in order to defer the tax.

How do I figure my capital gains on the sale of income property?

You will pay capital gains on any profit you realize from the sale of your property, and then you must add on the amount of depreciation you used up on the property. This total is taxed as capital gains. The advantage you have gained is that 60 cents of every dollar of this profit is excluded from tax. The remaining 40 percent is taxed depending on your income tax bracket. Also, a small part of the 60 percent exclusion may be subject to a "minimum tax".

Must I own the property any certain length of time?

Yes. At least one year. If you sell your property within 12 months of its purchase, any gain (profit) is taxable to you as ordinary income and you will lose the capital gains 60/40 tax, commonly called long-term capital gains.

To figure capital gains:

1. Sales price	$350,000
2. (-) Sales expenses	- 30,000
3. Net sale realized (#1-#2)	$320,000
4. Purchase costs including land	$200,000
5. Costs of improvements and equipment	$ 20,000
6. (-) Depreciation allowed or allowable	- 75,000
7. Net cost (#4 + #5 + #6)	$145,000
8. Net gain on sale (#3-#7)	$175,000
9. (-) Capital gain exclusion (#8 x 60%)	- 105,000
10. Taxable income from sale (#8—#9)	$ 70,000

If you are in the 35 percent tax bracket the year of the sale, your tax would be 35 percent of $70,000 or $24,500.

If, in the above example, you had used an accelerated or sum of the digits depreciation, those additional amounts would also be taxable at your ordinary income tax rate. The 60 percent exclusion does not apply to accelerated amounts of depreciation over the straight line rate. In some cases a small minimum tax might be due on the 60 percent exclusion ($105,000 exclusion), so check that out with your accountant.

Suppose I sell my property on contract?

The gain on an installment sale is taxable only on the amount of principal received each year. That amount is taxed as capital gains. The interest you might receive is taxable as ordinary income. This is one reason why sellers don't want a high interest rate. They come out better with a higher price for the building and a lower interest rate because the higher price is taxed as capital gains.

If you sold your 12-unit building for $350,000 on contract, with $50,000 down at 10 percent interest, your payments received on a $300,000 mortgage (held by you) and amortized over 25 years, (with a five-year balloon note) would be $2,726.10 per month. The schedule would be as follows:

Year	Principal	Interest	Balance
1	$2,841.95	$29,872.15	$297,158.95
2	$3,138.60	$29,574.60	$294,020.35
3	$3,467.22	$29,245.98	$290,553.13
4	$3,830.29	$28,882.91	$286,772.84
5	$4,231.36	$28,481.84	$282,491.48

Assuming you made a profit on the sale, you would have to pay capital gains tax on the amount of the down payment (first year only) and all the principal each year applied to reduce the $300,000 mortgage. The interest portion is taxed at your ordinary income rate. You would have almost $30,000 of income unsheltered each year. If you are paying off a mortgage, your interest payments could offset some of that $30,000 income.

At the end of five years, when your balloon payment comes, if you have been able to lower your tax bracket, you will save money. Let's say that during those five years your income was high and you had no other properties that would give you the shelter of depreciation. But then, when the balloon note has come due, you have retired and have purchased some other properties and have some tax shelters. Let's compare the two five year periods and the difference in selling on contract.

Assume the same facts as the previous illustration of your property sale:

1. Sales price	$350,000
2. (–) Sales expenses	– 30,000
3. Net sale realized (#1-#2)	$320,000
4. Purchase costs including land	$200,000
5. Costs of improvements and equipment	$ 20,000
6. (–) Depreciation allowed or allowable	– 75,000
7. Net cost (#4 + #5 + #6)	$145,000
8. Net gain on sale (#3-#7)	$175,000 or 50%
of total sales price of	$350,000

Year 1

Down payment	$ 50,000.00
Principal received on loan	2,841.05
Total received toward sales price	$52,841.05
(x) 50% rate of profit on sale	x 50%
Capital gain for first year	$26,420.53
(x) 40% taxable portion of capital gain	x 40%
Taxable income from sale receipts this year	$10,568.21
(x) 45% current tax bracket	x 45%
Tax in first year	$ 4,755.69

Years 2 through 5

Principal payments received for four years	$14,667.47
(x) 50% rate of profit on the sale	x 50%
Capital gains over these four years	$ 7,333.74
(x) 40% taxable portion of capital gains	x 40%
Taxable income for the sale during these years	$ 2,933.49
(x) 45% current tax bracket	x 45%
Tax during these four years	$ 1,320.07

Note: Average tax paid each year was only about $330 per year.

Year 6—with receipt of balloon payment.

Balloon payment received	$282,491.48
(x) 50% rate of profit on sale	x 50%
Capital gain for year	$141,245.74
(x) 40% taxable portion of capital gain	x 40%
Taxable income from sale	$56,498.30
(x) 40% average current tax bracket during this retirement year	x 40%
Tax due on balloon payment	$22,599.32

Note: The $56,498.30 spans several tax brackets. Assume

that one is taxed lower than 40 percent due to retirement and some are taxed higher because of the size of this taxable income. Assume this averages about 40% this year.

Summary for All Years

Principal payments received over six years	$350,000.00
(x) 50% rate of profit on sale	x 50%
Capital gains over these six years	$175,000.00
(x) 40% taxable portion of capital gains	x 40%
Taxable income from sale	$70,000.00
Income taxes for these six years	$28,675.09

However, if you *sold this same building* in the first year *with no contract sale,* the taxable income of $70,000 would be taxed entirely in the year of sale. Assume the tax rate would average 49 percent because the size of the income in this year would push the income into higher tax brackets. Thus, the approximate tax would be $34,300.

Note that by selling on contract you have reduced your total income taxes by $5,624.91 and delayed paying most of this for five years!

What if I live in my income property?

If you live in one of the units, that unit is treated as the sale of a personal residence. You must subtract the cost of the unit you occupy and reinvest in another residence with the previously mentioned guidelines.

Suppose, for example, you occupied one of 6 units in a building that sold for $200,000. The $200,000 divided by 6 equals $33,333.33 per unit, if all are approximately the same size. If you reinvested in a higher priced unit, you could defer that amount. If you should purchase another rental building, only the unit you occupy can be counted for reinvestment purposes. You would still have to pay capital gains tax on the remaining 5 units which are not covered by the rules relating to reinvestment of a residence.

Can I switch from one depreciation method to another?

If you are currently using a method other than straight line, you can switch down to the lesser straight line method. But you cannot switch from a lower-counting method to a higher one without receiving prior approval from the I.R.S.

Does the new buyer get depreciation advantages?

Yes. Once you sell your property, the buyer can start depreciation all over again on the basis of his purchase price and using whatever method he feels is applicable to him. If you purchase a new property you can start a new schedule of depreciation from day one.

Suppose I make changes in the features of a building I own? May I depreciate them, too?

If you are using a straight line method and replace, or change some features of the building, you sometimes can claim these features under another depreciation method, over a certain period of time. This is sometimes preferred by the I.R.S. to claiming them as expenses and writing them off the year of replacement. If you were to repair the roof, or replace some windows or doors, you would deduct these amounts as repairs for that tax year because they do not extend the life of the property.

Remember—you are not trying to attract the I.R.S., but should be working within the guidelines provided and suggested by your accountant.

What is the difference between remodeling repairs and capital expenditures?

General remodeling or decorating is deducted as repairs. Examples of Capitalized expenditures which must be depreciated are:

- Adding siding over existing walls.

- Adding storm windows or doors where none existed before.

- Tearing down and replacing a new garage.

- Remodeling a basement to convert it into an apartment.

Summary of 1981 tax code changes pertaining to real estate investments

The following are some of the changes produced by the "Economic Recovery Tax Act of 1981" which was strongly advocated by President Reagan. These new laws drastically change our tax structures and tax planning or tax shelter concepts. They are primarily intended to reward individuals and businesses for working, saving, or making investments in their businesses.

What are some of the tax changes pertaining to real estate, starting in 1981?

The major changes affecting real estate are:

1. Basic tax brackets—starting with the top, the marginal rate is reduced from 70 percent to 50 percent on all income; which means that those people who were in the 70 percent tax bracket got a 20 percent break. The new maximum is 50 percent (and thus, the maximum effective rate on capital gains is lowered from 28 percent to 20 percent). After June 9, 1981, a maximum 20 percent rate on net capital gains will apply to sales or exchanges. It doesn't apply to any properties prior to this date. Thus, an 8 percent saving is possible.

2. Sale of residence—under the present law it is possible to defer or rollover the gain (profit) on the sale of a principal residence if you purchase a new, different residence 24 months before, or 24 months after the sale. This applies to properties after July 20, 1981 and is raised from 18 months. In order to take advantage of the six month increase you must pay at least as much, or more, for the new property. Usually it's better to figure at least $1.00 more for the new property over what the old prop-

erty sold for. Note—this does not apply to income property as previously mentioned, only a principal residence.

If you are 55 years or older the new law now allows a one-time exclusion of $125,000, up from $100,000. (Again, after July 20, 1981.) The $125,000 is excludable from gross income on the sale or exchange of a principal residence. You must have lived in the residence for three or more years out of a five year period preceding the sale. This also applies to married couples with just one time exclusion applying for both. Neither can use the exclusion again. Should they marry after age 55 only one of these properties can be used for this exemption.

What has changed with regards to depreciation? What's new—What's old?

3. It's best to start with what's old—it's all old. Only properties placed in service after December 31, 1980 apply under the new (ACRS) Accelerated Cost Recovery System as opposed to the old (ADR) System, Asset Depreciation Range. Changes apply to the straight line method (SL) and the accelerated method, eliminating the 125 percent, 150 percent and 200 percent accelerated methods; and also the component and sum of the years digets methods. The new methods are the straight line (SL) and accelerated 175 percent, but do not apply to those properties amortized (low income rehabilitation expenditures and leasehold improvements).

How does this affect personal property?

For eligible personal property (and certain real property) it is recovered over 3, 5, 10, or 15 years and is categorized as follows:

3 Years   Autos, light-duty trucks, R and D equipment and personal property with an ADR midpoint life of 4 years or less.

5 Years   Most other equipment.

10 Years Real property with a prior guideline life of 12.5 years or less.

15 Years Other real property.

Taxpayers may use one of the longer periods as shown below:

Property	Optional Periods
3-Year Property	3, 5 and 12 years
5-Year Property	5, 12 and 25 years
10-Year Property	10, 25 and 35 years
15-Year Property	15, 35 and 45 years

Taxpayers have the option to use the straight-line method over the regular or optional longer recovery period, or accelerated method over the regular recovery period.

For personal property placed in service after December 31, 1980, the prescribed accelerated method results in the percentage amounts of cost claimed as depreciation as follows:

Class of Property in %

Year Recovery	3 Year	5 Year	10 Year
1	25	15	8
2	38	22	14
3	37	21	12
4	—	21	10
5	—	21	10
6	—	—	10
7	—	—	9
8	—	—	9
9	—	—	9
10	—	—	9

Now that changes have been made in the tax system, real estate is an even better investment. As a result the returns to investors on real estate will be increased; however, caution should be employed when using any one method. Please check with your accountant or tax attorney before using depreciation, so as to satisfy your long term needs.

The straight line method has been changed allowing a shorter recovery period of 15 years, or if you wish, you may choose 35 or 45 years. Now you will have more depreciation paper-loss at a quicker rate.

How do the old and new compare?

Let's look at the old vs. new taking a previous example of a building with $100,000 depreciation basis (already minus the land) 25 years under the old and 15 years under the new:

---

25 Years

$100,000 ÷ 25 = $4,000 per year

or 4% depreciation
per year

15 Years

$100,000 ÷ 15 = $6,666.67 per year

or 6.67% depreciation
per year

Year	25	15
1	$4,000.00	$6,666.67
2	$4,000.00	$6,666.67
3	$4,000.00	$6,666.67
4	$4,000.00	$6,666.67
5	$4,000.00	$6,666.67
6	$4,000.00	$6,666.67
7	$4,000.00	$6,666.67
8	$4,000.00	$6,666.67
9	$4,000.00	$6,666.67
10	$4,000.00	$6,666.67
11	$4,000.00	$6,666.67
12	$4,000.00	$6,666.67
13	$4,000.00	$6,666.67
14	$4,000.00	$6,666.67
15	$4,000.00	$6,666.67
16	$4,000.00	0
17	$4,000.00	0
18	$4,000.00	0
19	$4,000.00	0
20	$4,000.00	0
21	$4,000.00	0
22	$4,000.00	0
23	$4,000.00	0
24	$4,000.00	0
25	$4,000.00	0
26	0	0

As you can see from the above example, you would have an extra paper-loss of $2,666.67 per year on the same type of property by being able to depreciate over 15 years as opposed to possibly 25 years or more. If you decided to sell after 15 years you would have received (used) $100,000.00 worth of depreciation which could be taxed as capital gains, 60 percent exempt, 40 percent taxable, based on your tax bracket—the maximum being

50 percent now.

What is the new 175 percent declining balance method? And, how does it apply to income property?

Those investors who wish to increase their tax shelter may want to use the 175 percent declining balance method, allowing them more depreciation in the first five years over the SL method. In order to use the 175 percent method under the new tax changes, you would have to have purchased the property as of January 1, 1981. You may not apply the new method on any properties purchased prior to January 1, 1981. On those properties you must adhere to your original method.

A schedule can be followed making the math much easier:

Year 1	12%	Year 6	6%	Year 11	5%
Year 2	10%	Year 7	6%	Year 12	5%
Year 3	9%	Year 8	6%	Year 13	5%
Year 4	8%	Year 9	6%	Year 14	5%
Year 5	7%	Year 10	5%	Year 15	5%

The schedule assumes property was placed in service in January. Slightly different schedules apply if property is purchased later in a year.

How do the new and old methods compare?

Let's take the same property, $100,000 basis, and compare methods:

Year	(SL) 25 Yrs Old		(SL) 15 Yrs New		125% Old		175% New	
1	$4,000.00	4%	$6,666.67	6.67%	$5,000.00	5%	$12,000	12%
2	$4,000.00	4%	$6,666.67	6.67%	$4,750.00	5%	$10,000	10%
3	$4,000.00	4%	$6,666.67	6.67%	$4,512.50	5%	$ 9,000	9%
4	$4,000.00	4%	$6,666.67	6.67%	$4,286.88	5%	$ 8,000	8%
5	$4,000.00	4%	$6,666.67	6.67%	$4,072.53	5%	$ 7,000	7%
6	$4,000.00	4%	$6,666.67	6.67%	$3,868.90	5%	$ 6,000	6%
7	$4,000.00	4%	$6,666.67	6.67%	$3,868.90	5%	$ 6,000	6%
8	$4,000.00	4%	$6,666.67	6.67%	$3,868.90	5%	$ 6,000	6%
9	$4,000.00	4%	$6,666.67	6.67%	$3,868.90	5%	$ 6,000	6%
10	$4,000.00	4%	$6,666.67	6.67%	$3,868.90	5%	$ 5,000	5%
11	$4,000.00	4%	$6,666.67	6.67%	$3,868.90	5%	$ 5,000	5%
12	$4,000.00	4%	$6,666.67	6.67%	$3,868.90	5%	$ 5,000	5%
13	$4,000.00	4%	$6,666.67	6.67%	$3,868.90	5%	$ 5,000	5%
14	$4,000.00	4%	$6,666.67	6.67%	$3,868.90	5%	$ 5,000	5%
15	$4,000.00	4%	$6,666.67	6.67%	$3,868.90	5%	$ 5,000	5%
16	$4,000.00	4%			$3,868.90			
17	$4,000.00	4%			$3,868.90			
18	$4,000.00	4%			$3,868.90			
19	$4,000.00	4%			$3,868.90			
20	$4,000.00	4%			$3,868.90			
21	$4,000.00	4%			$3,868.90			
22	$4,000.00	4%			$3,868.90			
23	$4,000.00	4%			$3,868.90			
24	$4,000.00	4%			$3,868.90			
25	$4,000.00	4%			$3,868.90			

As you can see in the example you would get more depreciation under the new 175 percent declining balance method. Component depreciation is no longer allowed.

What about Recapture?

Recapture is a tax levied as on ordinary income, meaning no capital gains.

Recapture works as follows for residential property (only) using accelerated depreciation. The difference between the SL method an' the accelerated method is taxed as recapture (ordinary income).

Let's take an example of $100,000 basis residential property (depreciated over 15 years on the SL method) or $6,666.67 depreciation allowed. You would be able to take 12 percent or $12,000 under the accelerated 175 percent method the first year. Let's say that the property was owned for five years and just look at depreciation and not profit on the sale or other related capital gains:

Taxes	SL	175%
Yr. 1	$ 6,666.67	$12,000
Yr. 2	$ 6,666.67	$10,000
Yr. 3	$ 6,666.67	$ 9,000
Yr. 4	$ 6,666.67	$ 8,000
Yr. 5	$ 6,666.67	$ 7,000
	$33,333.35	$46,000.00

To figure recapture you would subtract the amounts allowed under the SL method from the accelerated 175 percent method:

$46,000.00 175%
- 33,333.35 SL
$12,666.65 Surplus of SL

The difference between the two, $12,666.65, is taxable as recapture ordinary income which could go as high as a 50 percent tax rate.

The amounts of the SL method allowed in the example, $33,333.35 are taxable as capital gains; 60 percent exempt, 40 percent taxable at your tax bracket:

$33,333.35 $33,333.35
        60%   40%
$20,000.01 Exempt $13,333.34 taxable at
                                          tax bracket

All non-residential properties using accelerated depreciation, as well as all personal property and substantial improvements to the property using accelerated depreciation, are taxed as full recapture.

As an example let's take a commercial center with a depreciation basis of $100,000 and using the 175 percent method after five years you will have used $46,000 worth of depreciation. The entire amount of $46,000 can be taxed as ordinary income recapture and could be taxed at the maximum rate of 50 percent.

Caution should be used when employing the above described methods. Be willing to look at your long range needs. It is necessary to point out that if you need more depreciation tax write-offs, the accelerated method could be used and might be the best method to use. Get good advice from your accountant.

Remember that with the accelerated method you will be able to get what might be needed now and will be getting the deductions for a period of time (until you should sell) and are allowed this write-off interest free. You might be able to trade your real estate and possibly avoid the recapture tax. Of course you would have to carry over the total amounts of the used depreciation on the traded property.

The improvements will be considered separate properties and are thereby entitled to the benefits offered by the new accelerated cost recovery system (ACRS).

What has changed with regard to rehabilitation properties and low income housing?

Rehab and low income housing—buildings which are rehabilitated but retain 75 percent of their existing walls may qualify for the rehabilitation tax credit which is as follows:

- 15% for non-residential structures at least 30 years old

- 20% for non-residential structures at least 40 years old

- 25% for qualified historic rehabilitation properties

The credit went into effect January 1, 1982. If the rehabilitation does not meet the new rules, the old 10 percent credit is still available. If the credit is taken, the rehab expenses (not the structure) must be recovered on a straight line basis. As for depreciation, the basis of the rehab property (not including historic rehab) shall be reduced by the amount of credits allowed. The 5 year rapid amortization rule for certified historic structures has been dropped. These new rules went into effect after December 31, 1981 on taxable years ending after that date. The old 10 percent credit is still applicable on those rehab properties on which physical work had begun prior to December 31, 1981.

The new law affecting low income housing allows for 200 percent declining balance depreciation with an automatic change to the SL method. The amounts of any rehab expenditures qualifying for the favorable five year amortization have been increased to

$40,000 from $20,000 annually per unit in certain cases. It is no longer necessary for you to capitalize the construction period of interest and taxes on low income housing.

What is Imputed Interest?

Imputed interest is defined as a rate of interest that must be charged on all contract sales (installment sales) as per I.R.S. regulations. It used to be that if two people wished to work out a contract purchase whereby the seller would finance the purchaser (act as the bank), he could do so as long as the interest rate charged in the installment sale was at least 6 percent interest. Now on all installment sales the contract must call for at least a 9 percent interest rate to the contract purchaser. If, however, the contract does not call for 9 percent rate or more, or does not show any interest rate at all, the I.R.S. will impute a rate of 10 percent to the seller.

A special provision is provided for related parties involved with an installment agreement whereby the effective rate must be at least 7 percent or the I.R.S. will impute 9 percent to the seller. In other words, the I.R.S. will take the position that if the contract does not show an interest rate of at least 7 percent between related parties then the I.R.S. will charge the seller on his income tax return as if he *is* receiving 9 percent interest on the sale.

Why would the I.R.S. care what interest is being charged on an installment sale?

With an installment sale the buyer's payments to the seller are split up and taxed differently. All of the payment which is applied toward the principal which reduces the mortgage balance can be taxable to the seller as capital gains. Any amount of the payment from the buyer as interest is taxable to the seller as ordinary income. So, if interest rates were lower the I.R.S. would not make as much money in taxes.

Let's say that you purchase a house for $80,000 on contract with a seller. You put $30,000 down and asked the seller to finance the balance of $50,000 at 10 percent interest, amortized over 29 years. Your payments would be $441.50 per month principal and interest. This payment is taxed two ways to the seller so an amortization is necessary to determine the amounts that apply to principal and those to interest:

Step #1

$50,000 mortgage	$441.50 payment per month: principal and interest
x 10% interest rate	
$5,000 ÷ 12 = $416.67	the 1st months interest payment
$441.50	total payment
- 416.67	interest
$ 24.83	which is the amount of principal payment the 1st month which reduces the mortgage balance

Step #2

$50,000.00	original mortgage balance
- 24.83	principal reduction 1st month
$49,475.17	new mortgage balance 2nd month
x .10	interest

$ 4,997.52 ÷ 12 = $416.46 which is the 2nd months interest payment

---

As you can see, each month the payments stay the same, how they are applied toward principal and interest changes.

At the end of one year you might have found that all that was paid toward principal was $311.97 and $4,986.03 was paid toward interest. You total payments for one year were $5,298 which means that 94.11 percent of the first years total payment was applied toward interest, and 5.89 percent of the total payment was toward principal.

The seller would probably pay ordinary income on all the interest received (unless they showed a tax loss for the year or were below the minimum taxable income).

The principal might have been taxed as capital gains, 60 percent exempt—40 percent taxable, an example of which was shown earlier in this chapter.

So, as you can see, if no interest was being charged or was below the I.R.S. Regulations they would not make money on such sales.

How about special programs with builders and some real estate brokers offering 0 percent interest or low interest rates below 9 percent. How is this possible?

It's possible because there are people out there who are creative and wish to make money during hard times. Basically it will work as previously mentioned with the imputed interest rates still applicable.

Usually, but not in all cases, the seller will raise the price of what is being sold to compensate for the imputed interest rate of 10 percent. It is also important to note that with a 0 percent interest plan the property is usually owned in a short period of time; five, seven, or ten years, and thousands of dollars of interest payments are saved by the purchaser.

If, as in the last example, you purchased a home and mortgaged $50,000 at 10 percent for 29 years, you would own the home free and clear in 29 years provided that you don't pay more towards principal or make a balloon payment. So, $441.50 per month over 29 years means that you will be paying $5,298.00 per year, or $183,642 in 29 years including the down payment of $30,000 with $103,642 in interest. Of course you would not be getting the tax write-off of the interest payment as the buyer, but could save yourself a great amount of money on the $80,000 home.

Where can I go for tax advice?

A good tax accountant or tax attorney is your first step. If you don't know any, contact an accounting or legal association for a referral. You may also write or call:

National Society of Public Accountants
1010 North Fairfax Street
Alexandria, Virginia 22314
703-549-6400

In Illinois, write or call:

Independent Accountants Association of Illinois
251-F Lawrencewood
Niles, Illinois 60648
312-965-1119

You can also call the I.R.S. office in your area usually between 8:30 A.M. and 5:00 P.M. The best time to call is 8:30 A.M.
Some free tax publications available from the government are:

Publication #17—Your Federal Income Tax (for individuals)

Publication #334—Tax Guide for Small Business

Publication #527—Rental Property

Publication #552—Record-keeping requirements and a list of tax publications

Publication #534—Depreciation

Many other publications are available in book stores and libraries.

35 Quick Tax Deductions

Accounting and auditing expenses paid for business or rental property.

Advertising expenses for business.

Alterations and repairs on business or income-producing property.

Appraisal costs for tax and business purposes.

Attending conventions for business.

Attorney's fees for business.

Automobile expenses incurred during business trips to and from property.

Bonus to employees.

Bonus payment to lessee or lessor.

Bookkeeping expenses for business.

Brokerage fee to obtain a mortgage loan if property is used in a trade or business.

Burglary losses pertaining to business.

Business overhead insurance premiums for insurance that pays your business operating costs if you are out sick or injured.

Carrying charges, as interest or taxes pertaining to your business.

Christmas presents and other holiday gifts to employees or customers or prosects when the practice in the trade forces you to compete with similar gifts. Limit to deduction is $25 per person.

Cleaning charges for business.

Collection of income and business debts, expenses connected with.

Commissions to employees—for example those paid to obtain business.

Compensation paid employees and assistants.

Credit bureau reports and service charges for business.

Damage, in excess of insurance and $100 to property held for personal use, as a result of a casualty such as a fire, shipwreck, storm.

Delivery and freight charges in your business.

Depreciation on business or income producing property.

Depreciation on tools, instruments, machines, furniture, equipment, or apparatus used in work or business if they last more than one year.

Education, tuition fees, books, traveling expenses, if pertaining to your business.

Entertainment of customers.

Expenses paid for the production and collection of income, and expenses to maintain, manage, and conserve property held for investment, even though there is no likelihood that it will ever be sold at a profit or otherwise be productive of income.

Income tax return, fees for preparing for business.

Income tax, state or city for business.

Labor expenses.

Lawsuit expenses, if pertaining to your business.

Losses (except to the extent covered by insurance) arising from:

1. Bad debts.

2. Foreclosures

3. Loans not repaid.

4. Mortgaged property sold.

Office rent you pay for your business.

Office stationery and supplies for your business.

Ordinary and necessary expenses in your business.

Painting and papering expense, rental property, for your business.

Plus many more. (See an accountant for deductions, shelters, and advice.)

As you are probably aware, Congress is considering tax changes, some of which will affect income-producing real estate. For instance, the 15-year depreciation term may be changed to a 20-year standard-depreciation term. If that happens, an investor will be forced to write-off less each year, and realize less profit. Therefore, it's even more important now that you check with an experienced tax attorney and accountant before you conclude any deal.

Although changes will continue to take place, once you understand the basics of depreciation and the tax ramifications, as explained in this chapter, you will be able to incorporate future changes into your plans. No matter how knowledgeable your attorney or accountant, nobody can make your decisions for you. Therefore, you must learn as much as you can about the factors that affect your investment. If you need to read this chapter a number of times in order to gain a clearer idea of its content, then take your time and do so. Once you get a good grasp of the fundamentals, you'll be in control of your real estate investments—and you'll reap their inevitable rewards.

AFTERWARD
A Step In Time

AFTERWARD
A Step In Time

You've finished reading the book and now, we hope, are ready to take that first step on your way to financial independence. You are ready to invest in real estate. Almost.

Chances are that when you thought about buying this book you were already half-convinced that real estate investing held your best opportunities for making money. But you didn't just think about buying and reading this book. You bought it and read it. In other words, you acted.

Now you're in a similar position. Mentally prepared to act. But unless you do act, unless you take an actual step towards your goal, you might as well have never read this book.

Therefore, do any *one* of the following *immediately:*

- Figure your current financial status—your net worth—and decide how much money you have available in cash and in assets to borrow against.

- Underline ten classified ads in the real estate section of the newspaper for your first phone calls.

- Phone at least three ads of property for sale in your neighborhood to practice asking for information.

- Call or visit a real estate agent and ask for comparables on 6 and 12-unit apartment buildings in your area.

- Write your local credit bureau to get a copy of your credit history.

- Drive around a neighborhood you'd like to invest in; write down the addresses of buildings that interest you and stop to find out their owners or management companies.

- Call your attorney and accountant and tell them you're looking for some real estate to invest in.

- Re-read this book—especially the Preface and the Introduction.

You don't have to hestitate until you know more or read more. After all, you're not signing a contract. And even if you were, you can look up the out-clauses to use for your protection. So what you need to do is get accustomed to the physical actions connected with real estate investing: looking, phoning, figuring, talking. The more you do, the more comfortable you'll feel with the process. You need to inspect some buildings, and then re-read those chapters that discuss what to look for. And then in-spect some more buildings. You need to have actual experiences to go with your reading experience. You can't buy property from a book. Not even from the real estate agent's listing book.

The hardest step of all is the first step in any new venture. You may feel a little wobbly, a little unsure on your first phone call, your first property inspection, but you'll feel less wobbly and more confident on each successive one. And you have this book to jog your memory, to supply the checklists, and to en-courage your next venture. Remember, once you take that first step, we'll be with you every step of the way.